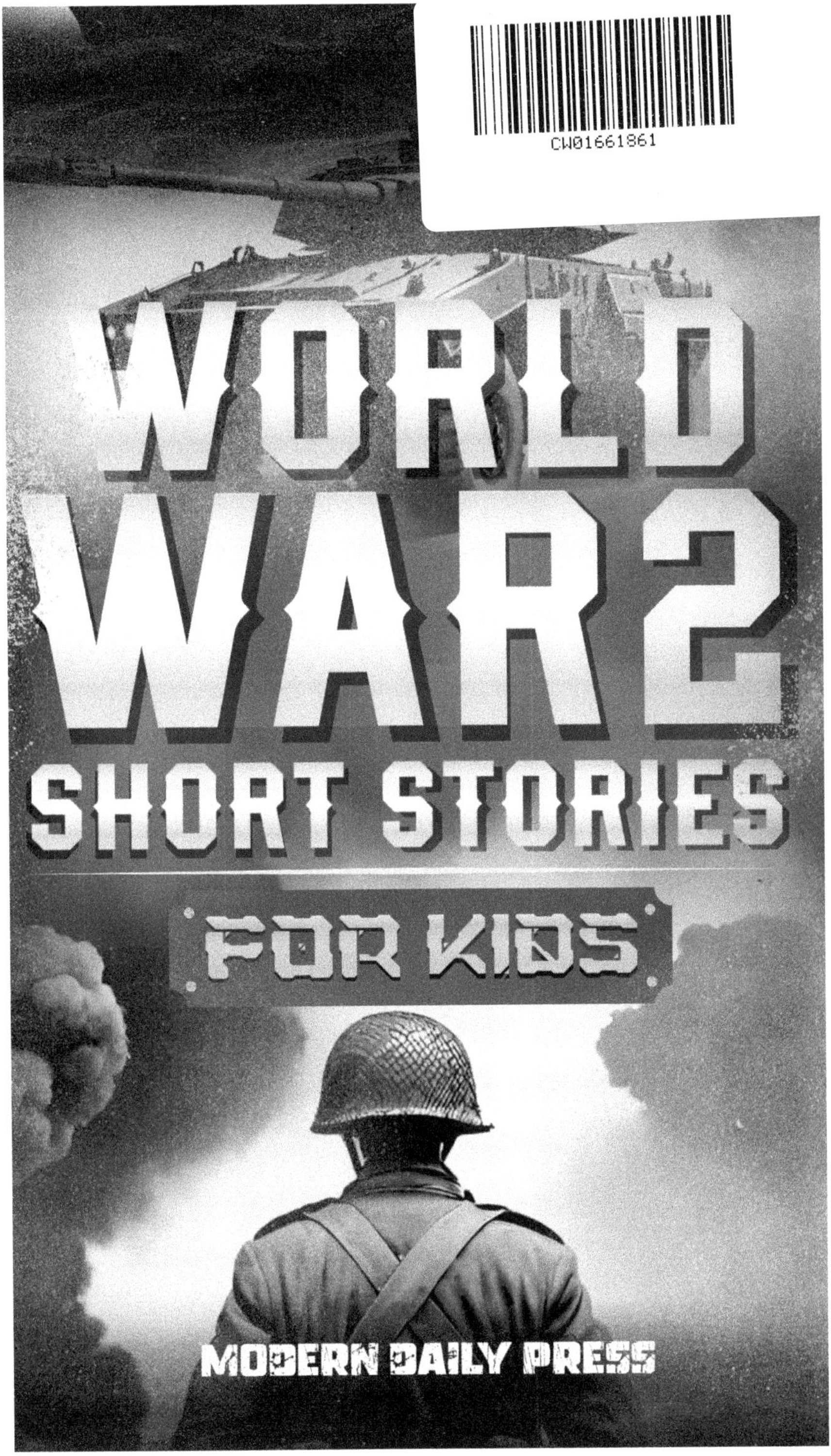
WORLD
WAR 2
SHORT STORIES
FOR KIDS
MODERN DAILY PRESS

WORLD WAR 2

SHORT STORIES

FOR KIDS

MODERN DAILY PRESS

World War 2 Short Stories for Kids

Unbelievable Historical True Tales of Timeline, Combatants and Military Operations to Inspire Courage for Young Readers

modern daily PRESS

BONUS DOWNLOADS INCLUDED

Download 3 Free Books As Our Bonus Content

What You'll Get:

YES, SEND ME THE FREE BOOKS!

Scan Here for Bonus Downloads

No Purchase • Instant Access • Safe Download

Dedication

This book is for kids who want to be reminded to be careful and vigilant because of how cruel the world is. Be the change to make this world better and not repeat the mistakes of the past.

CONTENTS

INTRODUCTION

> *"The world must know what happened, and never forget."*
>
> *- Dwight Eisenhower*

In 1918, the Allies, mainly Britain, France, and the US, won World War I against Germany. It was quiet until Adolf Hitler became the leader of Germany in 1933. Soon, he transformed into a dictator.

In September 1939, the Allies declared war against Germany after Hitler invaded a part of Poland from the west.

It was the start of World War II.

This book, World War II Short Stories for Kids, is a collection of stories that tell a part of world history. The stories included are widely used today to inspire the youth, participate in global discussions, and initiate and maintain peace. Wars have taken many lives, and this book aims to prevent any more global conflict by fueling empathy within us all.

This book will make readers feel for the majority of the population involved, the most vulnerable ones. It is divided into three parts. While the stories touch on various values and lessons, every part has its focus. The first part focuses on Courage and Resistance. It includes The Miracle of Dunkirk, Anne Frank: A Diary of Hope, The Navajo Code Talkers, Operation Anthropoid: The Assassination of Reinhard Heydrich, and The Warsaw Ghetto Uprising.

The second part aims to showcase the innovation and contributions of people from various backgrounds during the war. It includes The Kindertransport: Rescuing Children from the Nazis, The Tuskegee Airmen: Breaking Barriers in the Sky, The Battle of Britain: Defending the Skies, and The Women of Bletchley Park: Codebreakers Extraordinaire.

Both parts one and two have stories that took place at an early stage of the war or even right before the war was declared. Both have stories about protests, the sacrifice of ordinary men, and the marginalized sectors taking part in fighting for the nations using skills and intelligence.

And lastly, to talk about Impact essentially, I included The Atomic Bombings of Hiroshima and Nagasaki, which also ended World War II.

Brace yourself, and let's proceed to our first story, which took place on the beaches of France.

PART ONE

COURAGE AND RESISTANCE

1

THE MIRACLE OF DUNKIRK

> *"My humanity is bound up in yours, for we can only be human together."*
>
> *— Desmond Tutu*

Survival in war is rarely achieved through individual strength and determination alone. It is the spirit of camaraderie and shared humanity that sustains people. By empathizing with one another—sharing emotions, pain, and hope—courage can fire up to endure, resist, and face odd and harrowing situations.

❋ Operation Dynamo spanned from May 26 to June 4, 1940

❋ Coastal Town of Dunkirk, France

THE EVACUATION PLAN BEGINS

The German Army made its way through France and Belgium with remarkable speed. The British Army and other Allied troops retreated to the coastal town of Dunkirk, France.

The Allied soldiers stayed low and alert to their surroundings.

"The Germans were lightning fast," one of them said, sitting beside his comrade.

His comrade pulled a small family photo from his pocket. "I know this won't end soon," he said quietly. "But I just hope my family survives. I hope we survive this war."

Patting his back, the other replied, "We'll be home soon."

It was May 1940—nine months after unresolved tensions from World War I reignited. It had been 20 years of uneasy peace. Germany had been crafting warplanes during this hiatus to support the ground military. It was really up to something.

In the third quarter of 1939, German dictator Adolf Hitler ordered the invasion of Poland despite peace initiatives. The global conflict soon escalated, pitting the

Axis Powers—Germany, Italy, and Japan—against the Allies: France, Britain, the US, the Soviet Union, and China. World War II had begun.

Thousands of troops gathered in the coastal town of Dunkirk as officers relayed the new plan.

"We've managed to repair a few telephone lines, but ongoing fire attacks keep destroying them," a senior officer approached and announced. "With that in mind, we're now relying on radio communication. A plan has just come through—it's Operation Dynamo. Vice-Admiral Bertram Ramsay is leading the evacuation."

"He led the successful blockage of German submarines in the Dover Channel," a soldier added.

"Remember, we outnumbered the German infantry, and their approach has been studied," the senior officer is trying to uplift their morale. "They had no initial detailed plans of attack. Instead, they focused on quickly breaching our lines. They cut our communications and crippled our transportation."

"Their strategy worked. They split us into smaller groups, then targeted the weakest first," one soldier commented.

"Exactly," the senior officer acknowledged. "They avoided the heavily fortified Maginot Line, which we heavily fortified. Instead, they moved through the thick Ardennes Forest, then down the Somme Valley."

"The next thing we know, we're here trapped, fearing annihilation," another soldier said.

There was a pause.

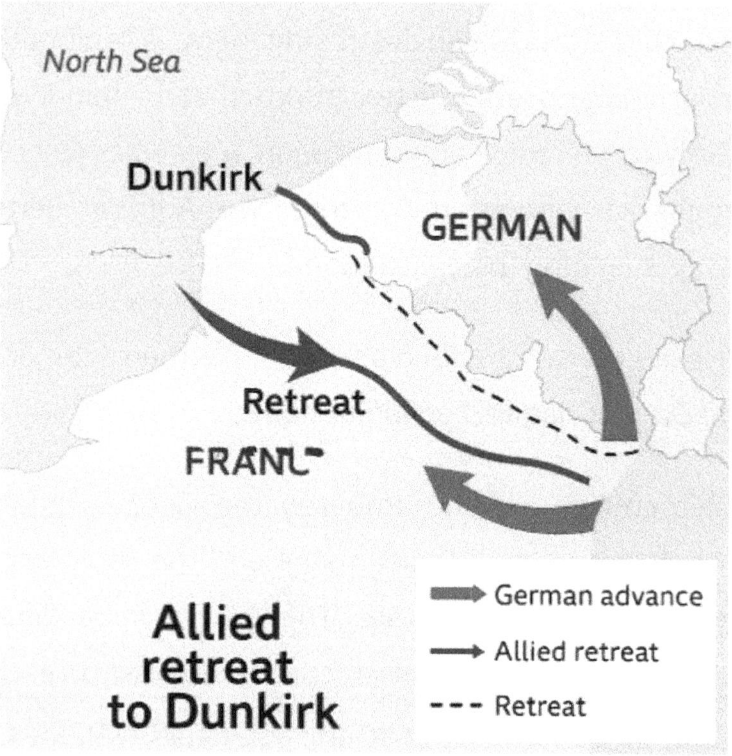

The German Army went through the thick Ardennes forest, avoiding strong Allied defenses in Maginot. They disoriented the Allied troops, causing them to scatter—some into Belgium, others deeper into France. The Germans then surrounded the remaining forces in the area, forcing them to regroup. With no other way out, the Allies headed for the French coast at Dunkirk.

"Being cornered here in Dunkirk puts us in serious danger. We have nowhere else to go. We're getting evacuated by sea," the senior officer concluded.

PERILOUS JOURNEY ACROSS THE CHANNEL

Despite the evacuation plan for the Allied troops trapped in Dunkirk, the British government struggled with execution due to a shortage of ships to transport thousands across the English Channel.

It was estimated that only 45,000 soldiers could be evacuated in the first two days with the resources available. Aware of the dire situation, civilians stepped in. Over 1,000 private vessels—from fishing boats to ferries, sailboats, and yachts—joined Operation Dynamo, with Royal Navy crews piloting many of them.

They were called the "Little Ships."

Their role was vital—large vessels couldn't reach the shore to pick up waiting Allied soldiers during low tide. The Little Ships ferried troops from the beaches to deeper waters, where larger ships could transport them across the English Channel to England.

Days before Operation Dynamo commenced, the German army was ordered to halt, likely due to uncertainty within the military leadership. They suspected the Allies might be preparing a counterattack.

Confused by the lack of resistance, they hesitated, unable to understand why their strategy hadn't been effectively challenged earlier.

They were still insecure about their small number. Concerned about maintaining their formation, the frontline units slowed down. They didn't realize that this pause would give the Allies a crucial window to prepare for and carry out the evacuation.

Soon, the Germans were back in the game.

Despite the British government's initiative and French forces' delaying actions against German attacks to ensure uninterrupted evacuation, the Dunkirk operation to England was anything but smooth.

The German Army tightened their encirclement of Dunkirk kilometer by kilometer. Simultaneously, German aircraft directly impeded the evacuation, engaging in aerial combat and bombing. Burning tanks caused by both air attacks and self-destruction generated thick smoke. It severely reduced visibility across the battlefield for both Allied and German forces. While this obscured Allied targets from German planes, it also hampered the German air attacks.

Small vessels, the "little ships," were loaded for transfer

to larger ships. Their increasing weight visibly caused them to sink lower with each soldier boarding.

"Leave your arms behind!" an officer commanded.

This risky decision forced soldiers to abandon their weapons to lighten the load and maximize the number of soldiers rescued per boat and eventually per warship. There was so much effort and camaraderie. However, limited resources, time, and harsh conditions severely challenged the evacuation.

The German army invaded Luxembourg earlier on May 10 and the Netherlands just four days later. Additionally, while the attacks and evacuation efforts at Dunkirk were underway, the enemy had also occupied Belgium. This news further demoralized the Allied forces at Dunkirk.

"We don't even know if our turn to be ferried by the ships will come," one soldier in combat said anxiously.

"The thought is killing me. I can't get my hopes up," another soldier said as he shot at enemy aircraft with his rifle.

CIVILIAN HEROISM AMIDST CHAOS

Luckily, the sea was calm, and there was no strong wind during the operation. The low-altitude clouds above the sea hindered German planes from effectively targeting British and French warships.

Many soldiers took another route: a narrow path at a harbor mole acting as a breakwater in one part of Dunkirk. It was an alternative to waiting in line for rescue by the little ships.

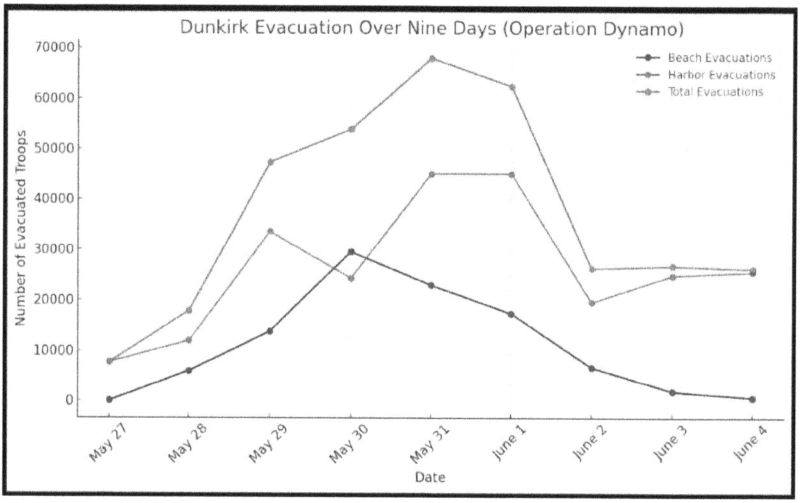

This graph shows the daily number of rescued soldiers during the nine-day evacuation at Dunkirk, and the path they took. More soldiers chose traversing the narrow path at the harbor over waiting at the beach.

A soldier found a piece of scrap paper on the sand and reached for it. He took a pen from his pocket and wrote: "Please find another. Make a new life with somebody else if you can."

He folded it and placed it in his pocket.

"Last will?" another soldier crawled behind a tank and sat with him.

"It's for my wife. I have a hunch I won't return home alive," the soldier answered. "Maybe, won't even step foot on any of those little ships or the larger British or French naval ships."

"I understand. We especially acknowledge the Allied governments' efforts and even the civilians sent in their private boats. Still, the uncertainty of survival is just unnerving."

Many aircraft were burning and falling off.

At the end of the nine-day operation, 338,226 soldiers were evacuated, approximately 140,000 French and Belgian.

Many were killed, and many others did not reach the rescue vessels.10 It was chaos. The rescued soldiers felt relief as their transport moved toward England.

The soldier who wrote a letter to his wife was holding the scrap paper.

The same soldier he had talked to before approached him again, "So?"

The married soldier laughed and released the paper into the sea. What was in it no longer mattered.

Other soldiers, some injured, who had previously exhibited both positive and negative sentiments, also made it to the warships heading toward a safe refuge.

Their faces brightened, though a shadow of apprehension remained due to fear of vilification. They were overthinking. They were worried that the nation would judge them as weak and cowardly.

Many made it out, but the enemies soon closed in on the French coast, capturing the remaining 90,000 living soldiers. It was a mental torture of thought, guilt, and the weight of their responsibility as military men.

That's why they were surprised to find their overthinking was unfounded upon landing in England. Instead, the media was highlighting the heroism and miraculous success of Operation Dynamo. The emphasis was on the crucial help from numerous civilians who lent around 700 to 850 boats.

News about the little ships were here and there:

Medway Queen courageously ferried back and forth, rescuing 7,000 men from Dunkirk.

The 14-foot-long fishing boat Tamzine, the smallest rescuer, also participated in the rescue.

The 20-year-old motor yacht Firefly sailed to the rescue under the command of Commander Bowen.

Several organizations with their own crews and civilians skilled enough to pilot their boats also received significant media attention.

Titanic Second Officer Lightoller sailed his Sundowner to Dunkirk and rescued 127 soldiers.

The London fireboat Massey Shaw rescued 500 men.

The Ramsgate lifeboat Prudential rescued 2,800 men. Lifeboats from the Royal National Lifeboat Institution also participated. One of the organization's boats, Viscountess Wakefield, was sunk during the operation.

The main topic was the celebration of heroism, not judgments towards the rescued soldiers.

TRIUMPH AND RESILIENCE: DUNKIRK'S LEGACY

The decision to leave and destroy Allied weaponry at Dunkirk16 was tough but smart. If they didn't, it could have complicated the transport, and the Germans could have used those to banish Allied lives on the spot or in the coming days. This made the evacuation smoother.

It definitely contributed to the triumphant evacuation.

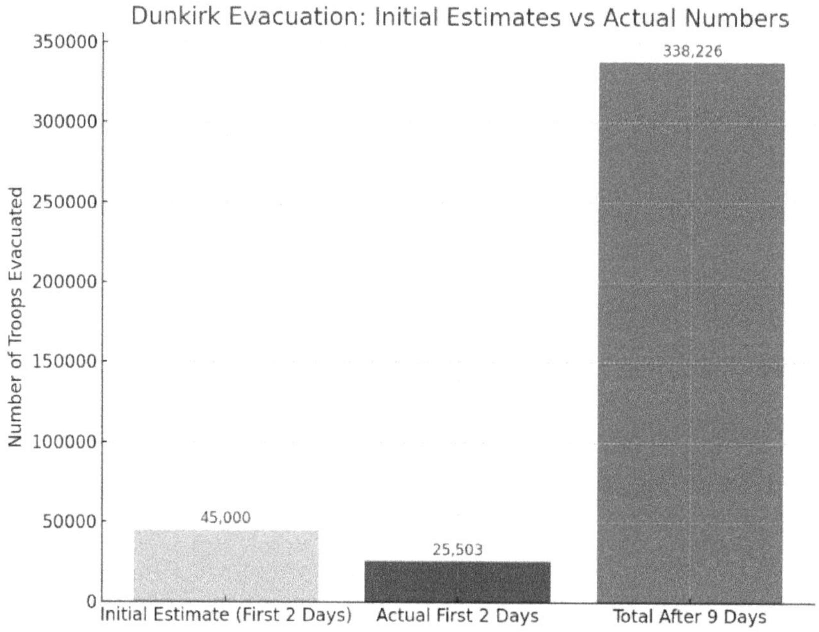

This shows the difference in the initial estimate of the number of rescues for the first two days against what was achieved for the first two days and the total after nine days. Despite the challenges every individual had to endure, surpassing the initial estimate of rescues proved a refusal to back down immediately. It was about pushing the limits and being resilient until they were close to triumph.

Another event that made the evacuation look triumphant was exceeding the estimated number of rescues. They kept going.

During this, many soldiers had to stay in the cold seawater for many hours, waiting for the little boats to come and get them.

Other soldiers had to protect the Dunkirk perimeter, covering for their already embarking comrades. It turned out to be a collective effort. It was sacrifice. It was hope. It was speed and strength of body and mind. It was offering a helping hand.

Courage and unity were clearly demonstrated in this World War II effort.

KEY TAKEAWAY

Lesson Learned:

Operation Dynamo testifies that governments that cared for their people and those who fought for their nations exist. Planning, engaging private individuals, crews, and organizations, and executing the evacuation under extreme war conditions was undoubtedly courageous, practical, and down-to-earth, respecting unity. The decision to prioritize rescuing soldiers over heavy war tanks and weapons demonstrated how the evacuation was centered on humanity, on human life. Life is irreplaceable, while material things are not, and the Miracle of Dunkirk showed how it's done.

Historical Fun Fact

Churchill's Initial Hesitation and Wartime Perspective

The new Prime Minister of the British government initially disagreed with and opposed Operation Dynamo. However, when it soon became clear that evacuation was the only remaining option, he voted favorably. Later, on June 4, while England celebrated the success of Operation

Dynamo, Prime Minister Winston Churchill cautioned, "We must be very careful not to assign to this deliverance the attributes of a victory. Wars are not won by evacuations." He then declared, "We shall not flag or fail. We shall go on to the end...we shall never surrender."

The Origin of the Name Operation Dynamo

The evacuation was code-named Operation Dynamo because it was discussed and planned in a room with an electric generator called a dynamo. This electric generator was essential in that room because it was located deep within the Dover cliffs.

ACTIVITY

Circle the correct word.

Can you circle the correct word?

1. The Evacuation of Allied soldiers in Dunkirk, France, was code-named **Operation Dynamo/ Operation Bertram.**

2.Many soldiers waited for little ships at the beach waters, while others took an alternative route along **a harbor mole/ a hanging bridge.**

3. The German Army sneaked through the dense **Ardennes forest/ Argonne forest** to bypass the Allies-fortified Maginot Line.

4. The evacuation at Dunkirk lasted for **nine days/ seven days.**

5. **Neville Chamberlain / Winston Churchill** was the newly appointed Prime Minister of the British government when Operation Dynamo took place.

Answers:

1. The Evacuation of Allied soldiers in Dunkirk, France, was code-named **Operation Dynamo.**

2. Many soldiers waited for little ships at the beach waters, while others took an alternative route along **a harbor mole.**

3. The German Army sneaked through the dense **Ardennes forest** to bypass the Allies-fortified Maginot Line.

4. The evacuation at Dunkirk lasted for **nine days.**

5. **Winston Churchill** was the newly appointed Prime Minister of the British government when Operation Dynamo took place.

2

ANNE FRANK: A DIARY OF HOPE

> *"The day we fret about the future is the day we leave our childhood behind."*
> *— Patrick Rothfuss*

A child, ideally, should be living in the present. Worrying is the parents' job. But, for Anne Frank and all the other victims of Nazism, a carefree childhood was cut short and was replaced by fear and uncertainty.

- In the hiding from 1942 to 1944
- Otto Frank made efforts to publish Anne Frank's diary.

LIFE BEFORE THE ANNEX: ANNE'S WORLD

On June 12, 1929, Otto and Edith Frank gave birth to their second daughter, Anne. They are a Jewish family living in Frankfurt am Main, Germany. Their roots have been in that city long enough to confidently say they are true natives.

In 1933, Adolf Hitler was put in position and became a German dictator.

"We must all join together to provide the building blocks for the new Reich, re-establish volksgemeinschaft – the unity of spirit and will of our volk. It will preserve and defend the foundations upon which our nation's power rests. It will extend its strong, protecting hand over Christianity as the basis of our entire morality, and the family as the germ cell of the body of our volk and state," Adolf Hitler firmly delivered.

Anti-semitism or hate towards Jews remarks and rulings had spread and filled the country.

"It will declare a merciless war against spiritual, political, and cultural nihilism. Germany must not and will not drown in anarchistic communism."

The chaotic environment led Otto to relocate his family to Amsterdam, Netherlands. This swift decision-making saved them from the Nazi persecution. Soon, they could settle in peace despite Hitler's threat to Europe.

Anne and her older sister Margot learned in school. The family learned the local language, Dutch, one of the great ways to immerse in the new community. They flourished and even built a business.

Anne grew up as a happy kid. She was known by family, friends, and neighborhood as one lively and inquisitive girl.

She collected marbles and loved playing with her friends in the neighborhood. But her favorite hobbies are reading and writing, which are good ways to keep oneself serene despite the continental scare.

The uneasy peace the Frank family had used to live in recent years shattered to fear, and plain uneasiness came May 1940. Hitler's order reached the Netherlands. Germany successfully occupied the Netherlands, and once again, after years of hoping for an okay atmosphere, the Frank family was under abusive government power. The Nazis didn't like Jews. Hence, oppressive and restrictive measures were put in place against them.

The Jews are ordered to register their identities with the

authorities. This is a big issue on security. In a dictatorship, registering with the armed forces secretly means that you are under watch and could be targeted easily at any time.

This greatly affected Otto's business. The Frank family leaned on the profit coming from it. Otto's strategy was to transfer rights to his non-Jewish colleagues. With this, he could maintain his role managing the operations secretly, without the Nazis suspecting.

Another among many other unfriendly rules was the segregation of schools. Jewish children cannot attend the same school as the rest.

With that, the Frank sisters had to part from their friends in school. They left and transferred to the Jewish Lyceum.

It was a painful event for Jewish children who now had a disrupted routine in the education realm. But with Anne's personality, she pulled off soon.

In 1942, the Jews faced even more restricting orders. They were told to wear yellow stars. The curfew was implemented stricter and tighter. There were threats of sending the Jews away to concentration camps. It was dangerous. The Frank family took it in all seriousness and immediately planned a way to erase their existence from the eyes of the Nazis.

It was Anne's 13th birthday. She received a red plaid blank notebook.

"How about I name you Kitty?" Anne ran her fingers to the cover of the notebook.

She used it as a diary, a diary she never knew would reach the hearts of billions around the globe in the generations to come.

The time finally came. On July 5 of the same year, Margot received a letter summoning her to work in Germany. It was forced labor, and it was the dealbreaker for the family. They don't want to give up their daughter to the call.They moved to a secret annex just behind Otto's business mortar and pestle the next day.

Anne's diary tells their story. While in hiding for more than two years, Anne wrote about her thoughts and daily life.

CAPTIVITY IN THE SECRET ANNEX

Have you ever played hide and seek with your friends? It's usually a fun game for kids of Anne's age.

But it wasn't the case at this time, for Anne was hiding not from a tag player but from army men with rifles aimed at her family, at her entire race. Normally, a kid playing hide-and-seek would giggle, trying to be undiscovered. But not this time. Anne's situation at the annex puts the giggle aside, at least on most days.

Otto's office is at Prinsengracht 263, Amsterdam. The secret annex had small rooms and an attic. Overall, it can accommodate eight people. The spaces were cramped, and the hallways and stairs were narrow.

At the secret annex, they were wary of being noticed by roaming guards and unreliable civilians, especially during work hours. Unexpected visits from friends even gave them anxiety. They can't even flush their toilets during active hours as the sound will attract the attention of whoever suspects. The situation at the annex was nerve-wracking.

Anne slowly walked to the kitchen sink to wash her hands.

"Please, not even a drop of water," Edith whispered, reminding Anne.

Edith guided her to a basin of water that was unclear from the other hands that dipped in there. Anne silently slid her hands in and scrubbed them.

"Quick," Edith pulled Anne's hands out and wiped them dry with a cloth.

The "not even a drop of water" caution impacted the group's hygiene. The lack of airflow and sunlight even added to their health issues. They had limited medicine and medical supplies but resolved these issues using alternative home remedies.

"Go, sit down now. No walking around until it's time for dinner," Edith refraining Anne from moving around.

They heavily relied on Otto's two employees, Miep Gies and Bep Voskuijl. They were trusted to bring them food and other personal and household necessities. The Frank family had limited time to listen to the radio to avoid noise, so the helpers also relayed news about what was happening outside. It was risky to help the Jewish community during these times.

You may be caught and imprisoned at concentration camps or sentenced for treason. Miep and Bep even had their own supply shortage problems. Still, they tried everything they could to help their boss's family.

Most families go into arguments, so what more can we expect from the occupants of the secret annex? They weren't just the Frank family; there were more: the Van Pels family and Fritz Pfeffer. They were miraculously surviving and getting help, and there was just no way that they wouldn't think twice about helping others, too, by letting them hide with them at the annex. Add to the population inside the cramped annex are the stress and fear they feel individually and as a group. Living in a confined space with limited resources and worrying about what was outside and what if they came in is challenging to their sanity.

Because Anne and Margot cannot go to school, they try to fill their minds and souls and continue their education by reading materials they can bring to the annex. They also try learning subjects and languages from their school books. Anne's love for writing was too strong; it didn't fade through rough times. She wrote not only daily accounts of what was going on in her mind and her surroundings but also short stories and narratives.

These activities contributed to the wellness of these two children, who felt normal despite their situation's abnormalities.

The Frank family and the other occupants in the secret annex also observed Hanukkah and other celebrations. They exchange gifts from their luggage or cabinet, but not newly bought things. Each celebration brought them together even more, despite occasional disagreements. Each celebration eased their negative feelings and thoughts. Each celebration was their quick escape, a break from their horrifying fate.

Although every day, everybody feared the next second of their life in the annex, they were never prepared for the worst, their arrest. In August 1944, the annex of Otto's business building was raided by the Nazis. All of the annex occupants were deported to concentration camps.

ANNE'S DIARY: A BEACON OF HOPE

Anne's family was well off in many ways, and the war and the German government's hatred towards her Jewish blood could have shattered her youth and youthfulness. But still, she wrote in her diary, "Despite everything, I still believe that people are really good at heart."

No one should be trapped in these mad circumstances, especially children like Anne and Margot. However, Anne managed to see the good in humanity.

Although the secret annex lacks airflow and sunlight, the rooms on higher floors, including the attic, have windows. Anne appreciates the joy and solace she can get from these openings.

She wrote, "As long as this exists, this sunshine and this cloudless sky, and as long as I can enjoy it, how can I be sad?"

Instead of focusing on the bad, Anne chose to concentrate on the positive. No matter how trivial it was, she was grateful as long as it offered a little something. Anne believed that people live to reach an end goal, and that is to be happy. We may not have the same upbringing, wealth, or experiences, but she believed we breathe the same air.

She wrote, "We all live with the objective of being happy; our lives are all different and yet the same."

And there is no pure happiness when you are not doing things to pursue happiness for other people.

She wrote, "A quiet conscience makes one strong!"

One time, Anne heard a radio broadcast that said, "We urge the citizens, please document your wartime experiences."

Amidst adversity, Anne looks ahead. She is wishful.

"I wish to go on living even after my death," Anne said, proceeding to rewrite some accounts in her diary. She was excited. She felt it was an opportunity to have her writings read in the future.

She was not detached from her family's reality. She was aware of the possibilities of survival and death and the fact that she could not control any of this at the moment. Little did she know that her diary would be the way to fulfill the legacy she wanted. She may not have lived longer to dream and live her dreams, but the words she wrote became a timeless speech.

Anne observed and looked up to what the people closest to her were doing. She saw how her family was getting help from non-Jewish men. She witnessed how her family let others into the secret annex to share refuge. She saw great people. She was with great people.

She wrote, "How wonderful it is that nobody need wait a single moment before starting to improve the world."

She knew that if everyone thinks and acts with bravery and compassion, wasting no time expressing these, the world will get better quickly.

For her, "In the long run, the sharpest weapon of all is a

kind and gentle spirit."

ANNE'S IMPACT AND ENDURING LEGACY

Anne's personal notes and views about the world and humanity have become symbols of going about life and leaving worries behind. They have been turned into symbols of resilience amidst chaos. In 1947, her diary was published as "The Diary of a Young Girl". Her words sparked hope that potential was seen and that they would inspire tons of kids and adults across the globe. And so it was translated into over 70 languages. Thirty million copies were sold and reached various cultures.

Her story was passed on from generation to generation. It has been part of some school curricula to let children understand the atrocities in the past and impart to them the importance of empathy so as not to repeat history.

Anne's story also starred in various films, artworks, and plays. Art transcends and is a great way to let Anne's diary live over time.

The Nazi occupation executed one of the most horrible things in human history, the Holocaust. Anne's diary became one of the representations of the lives taken in his dark era.

Her innocence, tainted by the injustice presented in front of her, made activists like Nelson Mandela seek proper acknowledgment of various human rights and deter anti-semitism and discrimination. For him, the fight is a struggle but necessary. We can't keep on losing innocent, hopeful, and courageous souls like Anne's. We can't keep on losing potential.

The secret annex in Amsterdam, Netherlands, is preserved and is open to visitors. Millions visit the annex annually. A real-life scale of the annex was also built in New York.

These are steps taken to remind the public not to forget how many lives could struggle and be wasted when compassion is absent and human dignity is disrespected.

KEY TAKEAWAY

Lesson Learned:

Anne's diary paved the way for the young perspective of the then-war. It was instilled in people across ages that the voice of the youth is valuable and must be given attention. It is fresh, brave, and full of hope, but at the same time, vulnerable. Listening to the youth will inspire adults to move forward. It will foster the urge in people to fight for what is just to protect, especially the young minds who are just starting to explore and make a change in this world. Innocence, honesty, admission of fear, gratitude, and bravery are good traits people can take from children. It is a unique lens that can help adults reevaluate and realign their values and stance. The light shines through the young eyes. It's just a memory away to say that everyone was once a child.

Historical Fun Fact

Otto Frank's service in World War I

Nazism disregarded Otto Frank's patriotism and service. Regardless of one's ties to Germany, Adolf Hitler intended for Jewish people to suffer. In Otto's case, this clearly demonstrates that serving one's nation does not equate to serving the officials in power.

The Concealed Annex

Have you seen photos, videos, or home designs with concealed rooms? It was the same with the Secret Annex. A bookshelf was placed before the entry arch to the secret annex behind Otto's office.

ACTIVITY

Can you fill in the blanks and complete the story?

Adolf Hitler set up discriminating laws against the ________ people. Anne Frank came from a Jewish family, and his father, ______ Frank, decided to bring the whole family to the ______ Otto was scared for his family. Although he served in the German military during World War I, Nazism was now targeting Jews, and he was no exception.

They found refuge in the Netherlands. Anne Frank and her sister, ______, could go to school again, and Otto had a business. But soon, Adolf Hitler invaded the Netherlands, and his laws were also placed. Businesses had to be registered, and this posed a threat to the Frank family. They would be easily identified if Otto's business was registered under his name. He ______ its ownership to a trusted non-Jewish friend and clandestinely managed its operations.

When Margot was summoned to ______ labor into a concentration camp, they didn't let her go. They know it wouldn't just be labor but eventual death. Instead, they went into ______ in a ______ annex ______ the building of

Otto's business. The ______ family and a man named ________ joined them in the annex. They survived with the help of Otto's non-Jewish employees, _______ and ______. Anne Frank wrote daily accounts in her diary that she named ________.

After two years of living quietly in the annex, they were raided and brought to concentration camps. Otto survived the perishment of his race and worked out the publishing of Anne's diary.

Answers:

Adolf Hitler set up discriminating laws against the Jewish people. Anne Frank came from a **Jewish** family, and his father, **Otto** Frank, decided to bring the whole family to the **Netherlands**. Otto was scared for his family. Although he served in the German military during World War I, Nazism was now targeting Jews, and he was no exception.

They found refuge in the Netherlands. Anne Frank and her sister, **Margot**, could go to school again, and Otto had a business. But soon, Adolf Hitler invaded the Netherlands, and his laws were also placed. Businesses had to be registered, and this posed a threat to the Frank family. They would be easily identified if Otto's business was registered under his name. He **transferred** its ownership to a trusted non-Jewish friend and clandestinely managed its operations.

When Margot was summoned to **forced** labor into a concentration camp, they didn't let her go. They know it wouldn't just be labor but eventual death. Instead, they went into **hiding** in a **secret** annex **behind** the building of Otto's business. The **Van Pels** family and a man named **Fritz Pfeffer** joined them in the annex. They survived with the help of Otto's non-Jewish employees, Miep Gies and **Bep Voskuijl**. Anne Frank wrote daily accounts in her diary that she named **Kitty**.

After two years of living quietly in the annex, they were raided and brought to concentration camps. Otto survived the perishment of his race and worked out the publishing of Anne's diary.

3

THE NAVAJO CODE TALKERS

> *"Listen to the voice of nature, for it holds treasures for you."*
>
> *- Native American (Huron) Proverb*

Native people are the closest part of a big community to nature. They listen and speak to nature; it's a deep connection. If the army had not chosen to listen to nature, they wouldn't have been able to discover treasures innate to the Navajo people.

- 1942, year the Navajo Code Talkers was established
- Participated in battles from 1942 to 1945

THE NAVAJO CULTURE AND LANGUAGE

Anyone who loves picking up new dialects and languages might find this story interesting!

The Navajo people have a deep-rooted and close relationship with their homeland, a spiritual bond. It is more than just caring, appreciating, or being grateful for what nature provides; it shapes their worldview. Their homeland spans parts of Arizona, New Mexico, and Utah in Southwestern America. Their incredible connection and respect for nature are seen vividly through their daily and ceremonial activities. It is also seen in the structures within their lands. They sleep in dome-like houses made of wood and earth soil.

Their economic activities mainly revolve around herding sheep and crafting, such as weaving and making jewelry with beads. But their connection with nature sometimes feels one way. They also get challenged by climate change and water shortage.

Navajo have one number that means a lot in their way of life. It is the number four---four cardinal directions, four seasons, and four sacred mountains.

In the Navajo community, women are given higher respect. It is a matriarchal society where blood, wealth, and familial connections are traced along the mother's lineage. Women in Navajo have the right hand. They are the ones sought in decision-making. Yes, women are in Navajo commune governance.

Just like some other tribes, they also have a rich oral tradition. They pass down stories from one generation to another. They also taught history. The goal was to preserve their culture over time. Language is one of the core identities of a culture, and it is one of the easiest to pass down since it's learned early and practiced daily, say through storytelling, within a community.

It is the same way with the Navajo language, Diné Bizaad, a language that is rooted in the Athabaskan language widely used by Native Americans.

But that is if you are a native. If you are not, it will be challenging to absorb its complexity since Navajo is a tonal language. This means that when one's pitch changes, the meaning of the same words changes. It will definitely be difficult for non-natives to speak and understand it. This became an integral part of a strategy during World War II to develop decode-proof code.

DEVELOPING AN UNBREAKABLE CODE

In 1942, a World War I veteran named Philip Johnston, seasoned by struggles and success, raised his hand to suggest how to develop a difficult military code.

"I know people who can help. They are the Navajos, native Americans," Johnston suggested. "I am familiar with their language, and I swear it's complex."

He suggested the recruitment of the untapped skills of the Navajo people. He demonstrated to the Marine Corps how the Navajo language can be a vital machinery. The military team, intrigued by the demonstration of innovative and novel solutions, gave it a shot. Twenty-nine Navajo men were recruited to develop the code.

The exchange should be flawless: easily memorized and transmitted from one to another and hard to decode by enemies. Enemies have good cryptographers who can decipher intercepted messages.

The team created the code with 211 terms.

"Okay, officer. Here is an example. We conceal tank with the term turtle," one of the Navajo men started demonstrating.

"Same first letters. Crackable," the officer commented.

"Definitely. So, we use our language," the Navajo code talker continued. "Turtle in our language, it is Ch'ééh digháhii."

It is not even of the same letter, so it will really be mind-boggling for a decoder. The concealing terms were words familiar to the everyday life of the Navajo community.

The military officer shook his head in amazement, "Unbreakable. Thank you. Please keep up the good work."

Once done, they underwent a test, and that included intense pressure training designed to simulate and prepare the Navajo men in case any of them gets captured.

What before took hours to transmit and decode by the receiver, the Navajo men did in less than 3 minutes.

That was how efficient the skills of Navajo men were for the war. Each of the 29 Navajo men were given bodyguards to prevent enemies from capturing them.

As the war continued, the number of terms for the coding increased to 400, to include the new equipment and weapons and plans and techniques and strategies.

More Navajo men were recruited throughout the war;

it reached over 400 in total.

The Navajo men successfully pulled their roles off. If not for the Navajo men's flexibility and great skill, they wouldn't have won that battle against the Japanese military.

DEPLOYING THE CODE IN COMBAT: BATTLEFIELD SUCCESSES

Aside from the 1942 Guadalcanal Campaign win, the Navajo Code talkers paved the way for secure marine communications during the Tarawa Assault. Navajo men could transmit over 800 coded messages without any lapses or errors. The communication was smooth and flawless, despite the need to coordinate the military across extremely complex water landings to fight the strong line of Japanese troops.

The same was executed in the Peleliu Operations in 1944. The Navajo Code Talkers helped keep the communication lines uninterrupted. This enabled the US army to learn the movements of the Japanese quickly through difficult terrain, allowing it to strategize real-time counterattacks.

The Okinawa Campaign had a chaotic and terrible combat zone atmosphere. It was fearful because the Japanese focused on getting in the way of the US operations, trying to meddle with the tactics. Luckily, the Navajo men were persistent enough to relay messages effectively, preventing Japanese interception.

The Iwo Jima battle also benefited from the hard work and natural skill of the Navajo men.

Six Code talkers worked continuously to transmit more than 800 messages, and like with the Guadalcanal campaign, this, too, had no errors. Despite being under constant fire and capture attempts, the Navajo men made it, keeping composure and remaining steadfast. Some of them had even gotten wounded. Under horrifying circumstances, the Navajo men kept their word of cooperation and utmost quality of delivery as to why they were there. Japanese cryptographers are excellent decoders, but the Navajo code was just unbreakable.

For more than 20 years, the Navajo code was kept.

This protection and proactive act, set in case another war arises after World War II, delayed the recognition of the Navajo code talkers. They returned to their homeland and, after being long exposed to the military environment, had to relearn to act as civilians.

The truth of discrimination among native Americans affected even the Navajo Code Talkers since they weren't nationally recognized, and they couldn't talk about being a vital part of the US Army during the dark years just yet. They had faced challenges, including work-related ones, and clung to societal pressures. Add to that the traumatic experience that they have brought with them from the war.

The Navajo men were finally celebrated when their military work was finally declassified.

"Were it not for the Navajos, the Marines would never have taken Iwo Jima," praised the signal officer from the Iwo Jima battle, Major Howard Connor.

Two of the named Navajo men were Chester Nez and John Kinsel Jr..

The Navajo men proved how skilled and resilient they were. Even though their operations training was short, they executed the mission excellently. They were also proud of their achievements, yet their humility made everything about them, including their dedication, even more admirable. Their legacy brought the whole native Navajo community to the peak of being honorable people.

RECOGNITION AND POST WAR LEGACY

The enduring legacy of the Navajo men spanned across nations and generations. It resonated beyond the years of World War II. Their bravery and intelligence were widely appreciated that August 14 is even observed annually to commemorate their heroism.

In 2000, the US Congress honored the First Twenty-Nine Navajo Code Talkers with the Congressional Gold Medal, one of America's most significant and prestigious awards and honors. After the first 29, the other recruited Navajo men were also bestowed and honored with the Congressional Silver Medal the following year.

The Navajo men changed the views of many in the global population. It was a profound change in perspective that even the Navajo community, especially the children, gained back their pride and trust in what they could do for humanity. Their legacy clearly imparted that anyone can be a national asset, emerge from any community, regardless of size, origin, and cultural identity, take action, and take the brave step to save millions of lives. People were drawn to their language, and this interest uplifted the Navajo community's pride. The legendary story of the Navajo code talkers was passed on to the next generations, the young

Navajos and others outside the community, to inspire and give courage.

Many schools share the story with their students, hoping to impart and instill in them the values the Navajo men possessed. The story's unique texture and heroism attracted millions of listening ears.

Cultural centers and museums were built to preserve and commemorate the Navajo men's greatness and the Navajo community's cultural identity. These establishments are great instruments that let people remember the importance of the Navajo code talkers' contribution to the world. They played a big part in bringing the Allied forces to victory.

Last October 2024, one of the original 29 Navajo code talkers, John Kinsel Jr., died. At the age of 107, people around the globe paid respects. They once again revisited the wartime and the Navajo men's selfless and dedicated service that freed humanity from cruel invasions and occupations.

KEY TAKEAWAY

Lesson Learned:

We shouldn't belittle anyone and serve as the voice of the marginalized. The Navajo community, being an indigenous group, was discriminated against and not given the equal opportunity and protection that every human deserved. Their skill in being tapped and recognized by military officials was a big step in firing their patriotism and self-esteem. It is important to value diversity, to let people from various backgrounds get into the system, and to build connections that can lead to creative solutions, in this case, the genesis of the unbreakable codes that actually saved lives. We can never know who among us just needs a little push to spark something that can improve the world. So many untapped strengths, intelligence, and natural skills, shying away or, worse, killed within just because the people surrounding them think highly of themselves and put these people down because of prejudice and stereotyping.

Historical Fun Fact

Initiative of the Navajo to create new words

The original 29 Navajo code talkers made the codes even more impossible to decode by not translating some directly. Say submarine. This word doesn't exist in the Navajo language; what's available in their everyday life that's close to describing submarines are iron and fish. So, it was coded as an iron fish.

There were other native languages used other than Navajo

Although Navajo was the primary language used to build the codes throughout the historical wars, other native American languages were also used. There were Comanche, Choctaw, and Lakota. Native languages played a vital role in wartime, effectively concealing military communication.

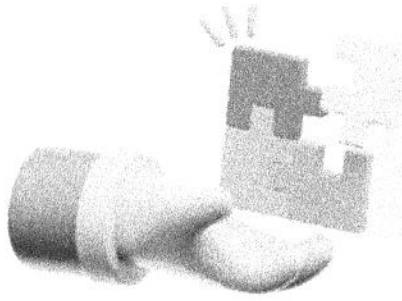

ACTIVITY

1. What part of America do the Navajo inhabitants live in?

2. What do the Navajo men call themselves?

3. How many Navajo men comprised the original Navajo code talkers?

4. Using the Marine Corps' usual technique of transmitting messages, even with the use of a decoder machine, the codes successfully reached the receiver for hours. When the skills of Navajo men were in the game, was a lot of time saved?

5. What award was given to the hundreds of Navajo men recruited after the original 29?

Answers:

1. What part of America do the Navajo inhabitants live in? **Southwest of America.**

2. What do the Navajo men call themselves? **Dine.**

3. How many Navajo men comprised the original Navajo code talkers? **29.**

4. Using the Marine Corps' usual technique of transmitting messages, even with the use of a decoder machine, the codes successfully reached the receiver for hours. When the skills of Navajo men were in the game, was a lot of time saved? **Yes, one message usually is received within 3 minutes.**

5. What award was given to the hundreds of Navajo men recruited after the original 29? **Congressional Silver Medal.**

4

OPERATION ANTHROPOID:

THE ASSASSINATION OF REINHARD HEYDRICHK

> *"A man dies when he refuses to stand up for that which is right. A man dies when he refuses to stand up for justice."*
>
> *- Martin Luther King Jr.*

In Operation Anthropoid, the paratroopers stood up to shake the system. Sure, targeting the Nazi military governor commanding their homeland gave them shivers. Still, it was necessary to let the Nazis know that they were also under watch. And so when the paratroopers breathed their last breaths, there were no regrets.

- May 27, 1942
- Prague, Czechoslovakia

PLANNING THE ASSASSINATION: OPERATION ANTHROPOID

In 1938, the German government occupied parts of Czechoslovakia through the Munich Agreement. This was agreed upon because numerous German natives were living in the country and in hopes that this would also stop the war threats coming from Adolf Hitler.

However, Hitler still pushed Nazism despite peace initiatives. It occupied the whole of Czechoslovakia and implemented cruel rulings64 under the mean Nazi official Reinhard Heydrich. How cruel? He was called "The Butcher". He made the lives of Czechs miserable, letting them live terrified every day. He was also one of the minds behind targeting the Jewish people.

Original Czech leaders were exiled to England, leaving the countrymen they once led. Little did people know that these leaders sought help from the British spy group Special Operations Executive or SOE.

"We came here to ask for help, Sir," Edvard Benes, Czech president in exile, politely asked the British Brigadier Colin Gubbins. "We want to assassinate The Butcher."

"Reinhard's assassination is also in SOE, but we still

haven't thought of how," replied Brigadier Gubbins.

František Moravec, head of Czech military intelligence in exile, convinced the Brigadier, "Maybe, with our information, we can execute this."

They wanted to do something for the people left behind and let the Czechs and the Allies know they were still fighting for the country. Brigadier Gubbins agreed to help, and they started plotting Heydrich's assassination. Moravec called it Operation Anthropoid.

Two soldiers in exile, Jozef Gabčík and Karel Svoboda, Slovak and Czech military officers from Czechoslovakia, were recruited to execute the assassination. They were sent to Scotland to be trained on various military weapons, to be taught how to trail and read maps, and to jump out of the air from a plane. But Svoboda hurt his head during training. Jan Kubiš replaced him.

It was assumed that the Nazis would hunt the hitmen down after the assassination. Heydrich was one of the biggies in that dark era. He was even best friends with another critical Nazi official, Himmler. So they also planned an escape. The escape will be possible through the help of trusted families from Prague who were also not in favor of the abusive Nazism.

Everyone involved knew how dangerous the stint was, and nobody really dared to betray the team, at least this early.

THE ASSASSINATION ATTEMPT: TARGETING HEYDRICH

Most Czechs know how Heydrich's day starts. He rides his open-top car to work in Prague, the capital of Czechoslovakia, with no bodyguards, just his chauffeur. He was lax, confident that no one would dare touch or give him a short jumpscare.

On May 27, 1942, the assassination was set to happen. The day came, and the two soldier assassins, Gabčík and Kubiš, had to face their fear, the man being feared in their homeland.

At a tram stop in Libeň, Gabčík and Kubiš patiently waited with sharp eyes, their palms sweating with anxiety. They had set up one Sten machine gun. They tried to be steady, careful not to make any unnecessary noise. They positioned themselves near a sharp bend of the road Heydrich routinely takes. Finally, he came. Nothing changed. He was still riding in his open-top car, carefree, not knowing that was the day that would mark his carelessness, being too confident wandering around Czechoslovakia.

Now, take a deep breath because what will happen next is intense.

Gabčík stepped out from hiding, making himself seen and taking the risk in full just to aim at the target bullseye. Shoot!

Silence. Panic starts creeping into Gabčík's veins. His guns failed to fire. It didn't work at all!

"Kubiš," Gabčík called on his comrade for backup as he ran away. Heydrich's car didn't pull away to escape. They saw how the gun failed at Gabčík. Heydrich seemed unbothered but pulled out his Luger pistol.

"N-no. Don't speed away," said Heydrich. "Halt."

Kubiš pulled himself together and threw a grenade onto the car just before Heydrich could fire. The grenade exploded, and pieces of metal sheets from the car flew everywhere. Although the explosion pained Heydrich, he still managed to bring his arms up to shoot, but the two soldiers already disappeared.

Kubiš and Gabčík, both hurt from the bombing they plotted, went on different streets to escape. Their fear had not ended after ambushing Heydrich. They might have successfully finished their mission, but the blind followers of Heydrich and the loyal army of Hitler might be just around the corner, if not a step away. And, yes, the chauffeur's behind Gabcik. Gabcik shot him twice, crippling him. It was a victorious yet terrifying situation.

They rode the tram to one of the safe houses.

People who saw the incident stayed low and quiet. To intervene, whether to help the Allies or the enemies, was a life-and-death situation.

The feeling of successful revenge and being able to give the Nazi leaders a warning or a message that they were not safe at all because the oppressed would be coming for them too any second were somehow overshadowed by the fear of getting caught and facing suffering worse than death.

PURSUIT AND RETRIBUTION: NAZI RESPONSE

Then news broke out immediately. It reached the corners of Libeň, Czechoslovakia, and the radar of the Nazi government and Nazi armies deployed in different parts of the world.

Heydrich was taken to a care facility to be revived. Unfortunately, the shards of tetanus materials from the explosion had already released fatal toxins into his bloodstream. He was severely infected, and the spread of the infection was impossible to stop despite medical interventions such as surgeries. One week later, Heydrich died.

The Nazis were enraged with what took place. Not only did they lose a comrade, they were disrespected. Their rules were challenged and overstepped.

"Heydrich was too relaxed," one of the Nazi leaders said. "We must not take our statuses as a default shield from attacks. We don't know how else these people can plot things against us."

"They will not be able to plan anything at all if we put in more fear," the other Nazi leader firmly replied. "Yes, we must be cautious. But fear? They should fear us, not the other way around."

The Nazis in Czechoslovakia raided Libeň. It was terrible for the Czechs. These were the consequences they had to endure for showing resistance. The German forces were furious. It was announced that the country is under a state of emergency; the authorities can do anything against the civilians. They checked on each and every Czech they encountered to probe if they were with Gabčík and Kubiš.

A strict curfew was implemented for everyone. Many Czechs were held captive and tortured. Men were killed, and children were taken away from their mothers. Women were sent to concentration camps, while the children were either killed or distributed to German families.

They mercilessly wiped out villages like Ležáky and Lidice, claiming that the villagers worked with Gabčík and Kubiš for the assassination of Heydrich.

Flyers with Gabčík and Kubiš identities were posted in the streets. Yes, with a notice of reward. The Nazis had been talking bad about the two soldiers, trying to make the people go over and trust the side of the Nazis.

Were Gabčík and Kubiš turned in by their compatriots?

Well, poverty was rampant, and one had to think selfishly for oneself and his family. Say hello to Karel Čurda!

Karel Čurda, a Czech sergeant paratrooper assigned to a different operation, thought it through and decided to turn the Operation Anthropoid paratroopers and the families that hid them.

"I'm sorry, Gabčík and Kubiš," Čurda whispered to himself. "I'm sorry, comrades. More than money, I was offered protection."

Right after Čurda confessed to the Nazi army that Gabčík and Kubiš, along with other paratroopers, were currently hiding underground in an Orthodox church in Prague, there was no time wasted. It was June 18, and an exchange of attacks happened in the church. The paratroopers were at a disadvantage. There were only seven of them, and they had fewer arms than the army surrounding them. The enemies were also emitting gas. But these facts didn't matter; the paratroopers fought all out.

"I won't let the Nazis get me alive," said one paratrooper.

"Same with me," said the other as he reloaded his rifle.

The underground floor started to get wet with water, and it was rising fast. The Nazis purposely flooded the area where the paratroopers hid. But the paratroopers didn't die from it. After hours of attacks, Kubiš died from gunshots and bombings, while the remaining six took their own lives.

Their families and the families that hid them were also tortured and killed by the Nazis for protecting the assassins of Heydrich.

LEGACY AND HISTORICAL IMPACT OF HEYDRICH'S ASSASSINATION

Many lives were lost during this time. If they were lost for nothing, nobody could say. But to sacrifice safety and lives just to let the whole world know that evil got to be shaken? It was a powerful insight. Maybe, yes, everything that happened afterward, the punishments, the killings, were the consequence of going against the abusive government. Come to think of it, what happened might be assumed to happen, but it shouldn't have happened after all. Who's at fault? Not the assassins.

The Nazis were still to blame for their arrogance, their evilness, their habits, and their abusive rules. It is never wrong to be courageous and fight life's horrors. The intention was to pull the Nazis' power down, to hurt their egos, to let them know that they were not the highest of all men, to wake them up, to fear them, to oust them. For the Nazis to do, vengeance was never valid. They have killed many innocent people before leading to Operation Anthropoid. Their cruelty cannot be perished through diplomatic discourse because they were already eaten alive by power. They were enjoying their authority. They enjoyed choking and ripping innocent throats.

These stories were being relieved through retelling because they should not be forgotten. The brave souls, the lives risked, the families that were separated, the children who were put in danger, and the silent protectors of the paratroopers must be remembered. Moreover, the lives sacrificed during the dark eras must not be put in vain. People of today should not have to go through the same mistakes again. No pinch of abusive traits should be placed in a position to lead people.

The Assassination of Heydrich was translated into books and movies for the public to consume. The story holds significant lessons and values. Telling the story in different forms will help broaden the reach of what history offers the present world.

KEY TAKEAWAY

Lesson Learned:

The Czech soldiers, who were recruited to assassinate Heydrich, possessed one-of-a-kind bravery. Just imagine agreeing to be fronts in an operation which, everybody knows, will end your life, if not on the ground during the ambush, then after a successfully realized assassination. It was a moonshot to live alive and free after this mission. But their love for their country and their stance to end abuse, tyranny, and impunity, their hope for a better future and a better world, made them face the calling. It was not just the planning team and the paratroopers' effort that made the assassination realized, but also the families who welcomed the soldiers into their homes to hide from the Nazis. Some might say the soldiers die anyway. What are the families to thank for? Their cooperation and loyalty to Czechoslovakia and their homeland brought hope to the soldiers. The act was also a form of resistance that showed great disrespect to the Nazi rulings. It is bravery and compassion.

Rumors that Nazis sought help from astrologers

During the search for the two Czech soldiers and their other comrades, the Nazi soldiers consulted psychics and fortune tellers, expert readers of the universe and of fate through assessing placements of planets. It was rumored to be included in the detailed book "The Assassination of Reinhard Heydrich: The True Story Behind Operation Anthropoid by Callum Macdonald". If true, this shows how Nazis were so scared of the power of resistance that they desperately asked help from a then widely believed to be nonsensical and not science-based opinion.

Karel Čurda's Punishment

Karel Čurda was searched and questioned after World War II. He was convicted and hanged for high treason.

ACTIVITY

Can you tell which statements are true or false?

1. Czech leaders escaped Czechoslovakia and went to England.

2. Lidice is the place in Czechoslovakia where the paratroopers and Nazi soldiers fought against each other after the assassination of a Nazi leader.

3. Colin Gubbins was the assassinated Nazi official who led Czechoslovakia.

4. Families from Prague helped Gabčík and Kubiš hide from the Nazis.

5. There were a total of ten paratroopers assigned to Operation Anthropoid.

6. The Nazis reacted very badly to the resistance by killing Reinhard Heydrich.

7. The Nazis were so threatened by the display of resistance that they also resorted to consulting psychics and astrologers to hunt down Gabčík and Kubiš.

Answers:

1. Czech leaders escaped Czechoslovakia and went to England. **True**

2. Lidice is the place in Czechoslovakia where the paratroopers and Nazi soldiers fought against each other after the assassination of a Nazi leader. **False. Prague was the place in Czechoslovakia where the paratroopers and Nazi soldiers fought against each other after the assassination of a Nazi leader.**

3. Colin Gubbins was the assassinated Nazi official who led Czechoslovakia. **False. Reinhard Heydrich was the assassinated Nazi official who led Czechoslovakia.**

4. Families from Prague helped Gabčík and Kubiš hide from the Nazis. **True**

5. There were a total of ten paratroopers assigned to Operation Anthropoid. **False. There were a total of seven paratroopers assigned to Operation Anthropoid.**

6. The Nazis reacted very badly to the resistance by killing Reinhard Heydrich. **True. They harmed many innocent Czech lives, falsely accusing them of being part of Operation Anthropoid.**

7. The Nazis were so threatened by the display of

resistance that they also resorted to consulting psychics and astrologers to hunt down Gabčík and Kubiš. Rumored

True

5

THE WARSAW GHETTO UPRISING

> *"Give me a place to stand, and a lever long enough, and I will move the world."*
> *—Archimedes*

A place to start making a change in this world shouldn't have to be up on the pedestal somewhere. In the Warsaw Ghetto Uprising, the planning and training happened in confined spaces, in hiding. Whatever is available can be created to make up for the missing arms, good knowledge and strategy, and a courageous and resilient spirit enough to stand up, speak up, and fight for the future.

- A month-long uprising
- Warsaw, Poland

LIFE IN THE GHETTO: OPPRESSION AND RESISTANCE

Under the Nazi occupation, Jewish people were sent to concentration camps.

"Mama, it's big!" a Jewish kid said as he and his family entered the Warsaw Ghetto. "Are we staying here? With all of them?"

"I-I guess so, d-dear," the mother answered, coughing because of an unwanted smell.

"I heard this is the largest camp in Europe," the father said. He held his wife closer to him.

Warsaw Ghetto measured 1.3 square miles. But this vast space was rapidly filled with the deported Jews. More than 400,000 Jews had to survive the oppressive measures in the camp. The Nazi regime put Jewish people into the worst state of living. The Jews were deprived of many things. They were subjected to much suffering. There was high population density within the Warsaw Ghetto walls. Overpopulation worsened the living conditions day by day. Multiple families were housed in small spaces. Families had to share cramped spaces. Everything from food, shelter, and hygiene facilities were inadequate and poor, made even poorer by extreme congestion.

The spread of infection from unhygienic practices was fast. The Jewish people were even deprived of proper treatment and medicines. The vulnerable group, sick and weak, the old and the young, had little to no access to medical attention. The Nazis were never satisfied with the suffering happening before their eyes. The German authorities made drastic changes, limiting food rations by a substantial percentage. The captives were intentionally starved. They became thin and weak. Malnutrition surpassed being an issue to be addressed; the Nazis made food and water shortage part of the Jews' everyday life as if it were normal. Their body, mind, and soul were all grayed, and that was the goal of the Nazi government, to let them suffer the worst possible suffering until it leads to death. These horrific scenes during World War II consistently degraded the victims, the Jewish people. But some captives had a burning fire inside them to resist the unjust orders.

Children were put on the frontline as part of the first silent resistance. Why children? Not that the adult Jews were selfish enough to set the children as bait; it's just that they were small and could fit between the narrow openings in the walls of the Warsaw Ghetto. During these times, they had to think collectively. They had to think for the greater good, and the children could imbibe the importance of their roles in sneaking in more food to sustain the captives. At least making a way to feed themselves to live could keep their dignity standing. The children were very important players at that time. The clandestine smuggling of food and other basic supplies lengthened the lives of many Jewish people.

It was a perilous mission assigned to the youth, but it was necessary. Children developed bravery to fend for themselves, their families, and the rest of the Ghettos. Mutual Aid groups were also formed to systematically spend scarce resources, especially medicines, on those needing them.

Another resistance made under the covers was teaching the Jews, especially the children, to use the Jewish education system, a system that the Nazis had long banished. The lessons were conducted in hidden rooms and basements, any area that the Nazis won't easily see or raise suspicion.

The risks of getting caught and punished were still high. However, the teachers didn't falter and continued with the advocacy, hoping that values and learning would spark hope for people to dream and look into the future. There were also art activities to help the Jewish people release their thoughts and feelings. Spiritual teachings were also in place to revive the faith of the Jewish people.

It was moral resistance. The Jews were courageous and resilient in relearning Jewish values and preserving their cultural heritage.

ORGANIZING THE UPRISING: WARSAW'S DEFIANT SPIRIT

Little by little, the silent resistance of the Jewish people struck something in them: that passive resistance was just not enough.

In July 1942, there were massive deportations to camps with extermination facilities.

"More people are being deported here in the Warsaw Ghetto," said the father. "We were trapped, only waiting to be deported to another camp for annihilation."

"Our suffering will not end if we do not try to end it ourselves," his wife replied, looking at their sleeping son.

The rumors of genocide happening soon led the Jews to plan an organized resistance. Underground groups were born, ŻOB and ŻZW being two of the most known. Everyone was afraid, but they chose to face their fears. Other smaller movements with different political perspectives, such as the socialists and Zionists, joined the larger groups. They were determined to fight the cruelty of the Nazis.

A significant problem was that they did not have weapons. And so they smuggled arms, mostly pistols and rifles, from the Polish underground. Luckily, Jewish people were skilled and creative and could craft their rudimentary arms.

The Jews knew where they stood when it came to arms. Their strategy had to be refocused on the terrain. They built a systematic connection between their bunkers, and more underground tunnels were carved out as hiding places and points of strategic fighting placements.

Many Jews who could still function and move around were game with the operation. Leaders like Mordechai Anielewicz and Paweł Frenkel trained young adults and children to fight.

Women also joined as messengers, runners, and fighters.

Unlike the previous resistance made behind walls, silently imparting banned teachings, this movement was made to be loud and noisy.

They attempted to get help from the Polish Home Army. They supported it, but it wasn't all out; it was limited.

The Jewish people felt brave at this time more than ever. Their despair turned up being proactive. They felt like they were their own army despite limited training. They thought this was one purpose, a way to maintain their dignity, fighting as a group.

They cannot die without fighting for what is right. They were even hopeful that they'd get through the battle alive. Their will to survive was now not only revolving around to survive a day, but to be freed from isolation, from the chains of unjust and evil treatment.

FIERCE BATTLE FOR FREEDOM: UPRISING BEGINS

It was April 19, 1943.

The Ghetto fighters were ready. There were 700 of them, many of whom were aged between 13 and 22. German forces entered the Warsaw Ghetto to continue the last strand of liquidation.

Although they were 2000 in number, they were taken aback when the captives violently attacked them with makeshift arms and grenades. They never expected it, especially from people deprived of food for energy. ŻOB, ŻZW, and other underground groups had emerged and surprised the Nazis with their organizer attacks.

It was a violent outcry, a desperate move to regain the rights that were forcefully ripped out by Nazism.

The Nazis temporarily retracted but soon came back with more weaponry like tanks and other heavy artillery.

Warsaw Ghetto was a month-long bloody battlefield. Poorly geared captives versus armed but unready Nazi soldiers. The Jews' only advantage was their knowledge of the terrain since they were the ones living in this huge Ghetto, soaking in bad smells out of lack of hygiene and congestion. The Nazis didn't bother checking each and every corner of this stinky place. Hence, they were able to plan an uprising. Street-to-street fighting had become very intense. It effectively slowed the advancement of German soldiers.

They were met with various handcrafted weapons, and one of the most powerful was the Molotov cocktails. They were exemplary at burning the vehicles of the Nazis.

The Ghetto fighters courageously fortified the bunkers with no signs of backing down. The civilians were also active in giving support to the fighters. They disseminated information and gave tips accordingly to let the fighters strategize quickly to counter incoming attacks. The bunker they called Mila 18 became the command post and the center of the armed conflict.

They got limited support from outside of the Ghetto, leaving them mainly fighting on their own.

The angry German commander ordered that the Ghetto buildings be burnt. This brutal retaliation left the ghetto residents with no choice; they had to leave their posts, making themselves easy targets of the SS. It was the Jewish people of Warsaw Ghetto's ultimate defeat.

The uprising and defiance of the Jews became a symbol of bravery and resilience against the dark forces that outrightly trashed human rights.

AFTERMATH AND LESSONS LEARNED: HONORING THE HEROES

The Ghetto fighters and civilians mostly died in the encounter. In contrast, others who survived, approximately 42,000 Jews, had to suffer much longer under the cruel hands of the Nazis. They were thrown to other camps, like Treblinka and Majdanek, faced the same struggles they had to endure while held in the Warsaw Ghetto, and were eventually exterminated.

The brutality brought by the Nazis led the Jews to fight back also with brutality. This wouldn't have happened if the German government kept everything peaceful in the first place. Bad choices lead to bad results, and the uprising that occurred in the Warsaw Ghetto was a testament to how bad the situation was back in the day. When those on the high pedestal abuse power, the people they rule upon might look like puppets who follow in fear of worse retaliation, but they have their own minds. Eventually, these people will fight for themselves, for what is right. They will revolt against oppression.

Jürgen Stroop's report was able to document the destruction in the Warsaw Ghetto and the resistance of its captives in detail.

It helped that they found a personal diary within the premises, too, an eyewitness outside the ghetto, and Warsaw ghetto survivors who escaped from the following camps were brought in for forced labor and killings.

The Warsaw Ghetto uprising news had reached the other concentration camps. And instead of fearing that they might end up dying, the same fate the fighters met, they were inspired. It sparked the same urge to fight within them, and they built and planned their own uprisings.

Today, annual memorials honor the uprising and

the heroes of the meaningful sacrifice. There are also monuments and museums built to commemorate the fallen heroes of the Warsaw Ghetto. Those who survived and lived after the war spoke about their experiences to tell the world that these horrors should not happen ever again. Their stories were told through books, movies, documentaries, and stage theaters.

Some survivors who were strong enough to remember and endure the battles again joined in some dramatic translations with the youth.

KEY TAKEAWAY

Lesson Learned:

The Warsaw Ghetto Uprising started with silent and hidden resistance, such as sneaking in more food to sustain their energy and establishing schools inside to continue learning about the Jewish culture, traditions, religion, and values. These things gave them food to ease their hunger and inspired them to relieve who they were before World War II. They realized that not doing anything would kill not only their physical bodies but also their dignity. The treatment they were enduring was far too much. Nobody deserved to be treated this way out of racial hate and prejudice or whatever reason at all. This was courage seeping through their veins. While many lives perished, the sacrifice was worth it to give the Nazis a signal that these children, women, and men were strong and were a threat. Just imagine how threatened they were to resort to burning an entire ghetto to win. The uprising demonstrated the human spirit's awakening, from allowing the very unjust orders to wrap them up to refusing to be passive, finally allowing what they genuinely feel to come out and revolt against oppression.

Historical Fun Fact

Underground Sewer as a Safe Tunnel

Some Ghetto residents and fighters used the sewer system to prevent detection of their movement during the uprising. These sewers lead outside of the Warsaw Ghetto, helping some of them escape when the Nazis burned the community.

Photographs from the Warsaw Ghetto Uprising

A Polish firefighter clandestinely took photographs of the encounters, a few of the few non-German photos available and documented. He was Zbigniew Leszek Grzywaczewski. He didn't tell anyone until the pictures were discovered mixed with his family photos in 2023.

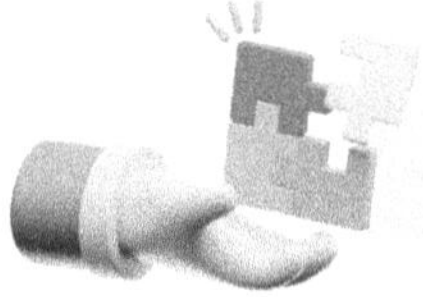

ACTIVITY

Complete the sentences below.

1. The largest Nazi-occupied ghetto was the __________.

a) Warsaw Ghetto   b) Grodno Ghetto

c) Stryj Ghetto

2. ________ were tasked to sneak in more food because they could fit between the ghetto walls.

a) Children   b) Men

c) Firefighters

3. The Warsaw Ghetto residents established schools in hidden rooms to teach _______ culture.

a) German   b) Polish

c) Jewish

4. The German commander ordered the ______ of the Warsaw Ghetto shelters to control the uprising.

a) burning   b) raid

c) closure

5. _____ and ŻZW were among the underground groups that organized the Warsaw Ghetto's violent resistance.

that organized the Warsaw Ghetto's violent resistance.

a) ŻOG b) ŻOB
c) BOŻ

6. Young adults aged _______ comprised the largest population of Warsaw Ghetto fighters.

a) 13 to 22 b) unknown c) 19 to 25

7. The Warsaw Ghetto uprising began on _________.

a) May 19, 1943 b) April 19, 1943
c) December 19, 1942

Answers:

1. The largest Nazi-occupied ghetto was the Warsaw Ghetto. (a)

2. Children were tasked to sneak in more food because their bodies could fit between the ghetto walls. (a)

3. The Warsaw Ghetto residents established schools in hidden rooms to teach Jewish culture. (c)

4. The German commander ordered the burning of the Warsaw Ghetto shelters to control the uprising. (a)

5. ŻOB and ŻZW were among the underground groups that organized the Warsaw Ghetto's violent resistance. (b)

6. Young adults aged 13 to 22 comprised the largest population of Warsaw Ghetto fighters. (a)

7. The Warsaw Ghetto uprising began on April 19, 1943. (b)

PART TWO

INNOVATION AND CONTRIBUTION

6

THE KINDERTRANSPORT: RESCUING CHILDREN FROM NAZIS

> *"Empathy is about finding echoes of another person in yourself."*
>
> *- Mohsin Hamid*

To empathize is to be sincere in feeling another person's feelings. It is putting oneself in the other's shoes. The humanitarians who initiated and volunteered throughout the Kindertransport mission displayed incredible empathy. They immediately took action to plan and evacuate children from Germany and other Nazi-occupied countries.

- December 1938 to September 1939
- Rescue of children from Nazi-occupied territories like Germany, Austria, Czechoslovakia, and Poland

ORIGINS OF THE KINDERTRANSPORT

Are train and boat rides fun? Absolutely—especially when the destination is a surprise! But in this chapter, no one knew if the journey would end with a return home.

Starting in 1938, the German government raised Nazism, targeting the Jewish people. Laws were created and implemented to discriminate against the Jews. They were stripped of their right to education, right to practice faith, right to thrive in business, right to have a safe shelter, and many more. Moreover, anyone caught to be going against the rules of the Nazi government would have to meet terrifying consequences. These abrupt changes in the political landscape put the Jewish families, most especially the children, in danger.

There was an unspoken truth behind the laws: whether one obeyed or rebelled, he would be banished sooner or later.

In November 1938, Kristallnacht, translated as Night of Broken Glass, happened, marking the declaration of war against the Jewish people residing in Germany and Austria. Jews were kidnapped from the streets, workplaces, houses, and churches.

Around 30,000 Jews were transferred to concentration camps.

Ninety-one Jews were killed, and Adolf Hitler's excuse was the assassination of a German Embassy officer by a 17-year-old Jew studying in Paris, who heard of the Nazis forcefully relocating the boy's family to camp.

Kristallnacht shocked the world. The terrible fate before the Jewish people put other people into thinking that there was something they had to do immediately. They had to intervene.

In Britain, concerns were raised from individuals to humanitarian organizations, such as Quakers, faith groups, and other welfare societies.

They recognized the need to save the Jewish children. The Jewish children were assessed to be the most vulnerable among the targets in this time of crisis. The children need to be relocated to safe havens. The key groups lobbied the British government. They laid out the initial plans for the evacuation.

These figures were really taking their advocacies to heart. Their empathy didn't waste time, but they immediately reached for support from the British government. From there, the Kindertransport was established.

One British Parliament official said, "Children under the age of 17 are too young and cannot survive without macro-focused support from guardians. "

"If we'd be able to secure guarantees from private individuals or institutions to have these age groups cared for and continue education, we can allow them in," replied the other. "Plus £50 for an eventual return ticket."

The youngest children were ultimately allowed to enter Britain, as there were people who showed sacrifice and generosity and promised to sponsor these children's welfare and education.

On December 2, 1938, 200 Jewish children arrived from Germany through Kindertransport, the first successful transport. The team continued to meet to carefully plan. They have to update strategies to bring more Jewish children to Britain safe and sound, given the challenges in the dark land of Germany.

JOURNEY TO SAFETY: ESCAPING NAZI PERSECUTION

The transport of the Jewish children was heartbreaking but necessary. Their families also had to endure being away from their young. The long ride, mainly train rides, that took days, from Germany, across neighboring countries, like Belgium and Netherlands, to Britain was filled with tears and loneliness.

The emotional strain from the separation anxiety was coupled with the worry of being taken to an unfamiliar place.

The children would have to adjust to the new surroundings and new faces. What's even more heartbreaking was that they'd be living the new way of life away from their parents, not for a short time but for a longer period, if not for the rest of their lives.

Kindertransport also rescued children from Austria, Czechoslovakia, and Poland.

During the transport, the volunteers that guard the children refugees were also under extreme stress. They had to successfully pass borders with Nazi checkpoints. Intense inspections were conducted using the travel documents per child.

Only one suitcase was allowed per child. The suitcase contained precious things that would remind the child of their family and childhood and comfort them in extreme sadness.

The children understand the situation, and they fear the war. They fear being separated from their families, but they also hope for protection, on top of the wish to see their parents again in the future, to be whole again in the future.

The Kindertransport had to cross the English Channel, which was the scariest part for most children, for the waves were sometimes rough, and most children and the volunteer guardians had not been in a boat before. They had to carefully navigate the sea within the Nazi regulations. These were also planned before Kindertransport commenced to secure safe passages to Britain. Kindertransport was able to evacuate around 10,000 children, mostly Jewish.

More British volunteers under Kindertransport had been very warm in welcoming the children evacuees upon their arrival in Britain. Some had ready foster parents, while some were taken to hostels and charity homes.

The British government knew about the difficulties

Jewish children might face when entering a foreign land. They would have to learn the language to adapt effectively.

"Don't worry. We will take things slow," one of the volunteers assured the children. We are all here to help you rebuild your lives."

REBUILDING LIVES: CHALLENGES AND RESILIENCE

To be immersed in a new culture while facing internal traumas from the previous challenges they endured under the Nazi government was a significant hurdle. They were promised welfare to better shape the future. Still, for these promises to come from strangers, it was hard for the children to set aside uncertainty and worries.

The private individuals and families who guaranteed sponsorship to some Jewish children also had their own stress since most were first-time foster families. They had varying experiences in nurturing children.

They had to overcome challenges like preventing bullying since there were natives who called the foster children names like "enemy aliens."

As days, months, and years went by, the war intensified,

and the children, who were trying their best to acquire English skills to adapt to the British environment while recovering from emotional distress, were once again filled with fear that their families left in Germany might be harmed.

Kindertransport volunteers helped the Jewish children ease their negative thoughts and feelings. The children strived to move forward until they regained hope.

The contribution of Kindertransport created resilience within each child. It allowed them to expand their capacity and ability to adapt. In fact, the children excelled in school. They did well both in academics and in gaining new friends. Even after many years, many Kindertransport beneficiaries have made outstanding advancements to contribute to British society. Their foster families were proud of their children's personal and professional growth and success. Altogether, they made it.

A Jewish child rescue, now grown-up, took a photo from his cabinet, "Mom, Dad, I made it."

His sister, another rescue, was at the door and heard him. She approached his brother and hugged him while looking at the old photograph, "We made it."

Remember when parents let go of their children, hoping

they would survive and be reunited after the war. Some were, but many never saw each other again.

KINDERTRANSPORT LEGACY: REMEMBERING THE CHILDREN SAVED

The kindness and compassion from various individuals and organizations that surfaced during the first years of the Nazi occupation became a story of inspiration. Despite the harrowing atmosphere in Germany, the British key groups and the government mustered the courage to innovate to rescue children from persecution. The mutual agreements with the German government to foster Jewish children was indispensable.

Kindertransport equates to humanitarianism. Its legacy is remembered through generations. It reminds the world that heroism can transcend races and homelands. The significance of humanity and urgent response to save lives and futures, especially of the vulnerable populations, in this case, the children. The effort to keep everything organized also contributed to a successful evacuation operation.

The legacy of the Kindertransport also continues to inspire contemporary efforts to advocate for the safety and protection of children worldwide.

Today, memorials exhibiting the innovation, contribution, and compassion of the Kindertransport are open to be appreciated by the public. They exist to remind people of the dedication of the Kindertransport to serve the oppressed during the Nazi regime. It is to celebrate the overcoming of the struggles while paying respects to the people who lost their lives.

These are significant testimonies to those who were given chances to regain hope and build a great future. The horror stories and the stories of hope of the rescued children are also taught in schools as essential historical references.

The Kindertransport narrative tells the importance of creating concrete steps to make something happen.

This also recognizes the sacrifice of the parents when they had to give in to the decision of sending away their children to keep them away from harm. Rather than keeping them under their wings, which were already set on fire, to stay together, the parents let go. Another hard decision the parents had to make back then was to determine who among their children would go first. There were limited seats to fill every round of rescue, and there was no guarantee that the children left would be rescued on the next rounds of help. It was agonizing, but they hoped for a better world for their children. Luckily,

Kindertransport did their best to keep their promise.

The sanctuary that Kindertransport created for the rescued children will forever be valued as a significant contribution during the dark times.

KEY TAKEAWAY

Lesson Learned:

In times of crisis, we all must extend as much help as we can afford to give to the affected. It's what makes humanity alive. Responding to human suffering with pure empathy and kind action is the best lesson imparted by the Kindertransport initiative. The British people and government's innovation to make the evacuation possible was remarkable. Kindertransport could transport thousands of children from uneventful situations to fulfilling their lost dreams by making everything legal and black and white. The collective effort of the private individuals, the institutions, and the government in Britain provided a very promising refuge not only to Jewish children but also to non-Jewish ones who were heavily affected by the war. The rescue that spanned across borders also depicted an elaborate and strong cooperation between neighboring nations. Finally, the children's eagerness to help themselves from being buried in the ashes of traumatic experiences is also very inspiring. If not for the healthy environment set up and created for them by the people who genuinely cared to rebuild their dreams, they would not be able to thrive.

Historical Fun Fact

Nicholas Winton, a Silent Hero

Nicholas Winton is a British stockbroker. He was in London, and he traveled personally to Czechoslovakia, in a German annex, to organize the preparation of 669 mostly Jewish children for evacuation through Kindertransport. He shelled out the guarantee money for the children in Czechoslovakia who didn't have foster parents in Britain. It was only in the 1980s that his efforts were known.

Some children thought they were going on a holiday vacation

Some children who hadn't really seen or realized the horrors of Nazism in their family yet thought their parents were only sending them away for a vacation. They were even confused when their parents gave them pieces of things as remembrance.

ACTIVITY

Can you match the terms from column A to their description in column B?

£50	The rescue operation that transported Jewish children from Nazi-controlled areas to Britain.
Nicholas Winton	The "Night of Broken Glass" in November 1938 that marked the declaration of war against Jewish people.
Kindertransport	The amount required per child as a guarantee for an eventual return ticket.
English Channel	A British stockbroker who helped organize the evacuation of 669 children from Czechoslovakia.
10,000	The approximate number of children, mostly Jewish, who were evacuated to Britain.
Kristallnacht	The body of water that Kindertransprot crossed and was described as the "scariest part" of the journey for most children.

Answers:

Kindertransport	The rescue operation that transported Jewish children from Nazi-controlled areas to Britain.
Kristallnacht	The "Night of Broken Glass" in November 1938 that marked the declaration of war against Jewish people.
£50	The amount required per child as a guarantee for an eventual return ticket.
Nicholas Winton	A British stockbroker who helped organize the evacuation of 669 children from Czechoslovakia.
10,000	The approximate number of children, mostly Jewish, who were evacuated to Britain.
English Channel	The body of water that Kindertransprot crossed and was described as the "scariest part" of the journey for most children.

7

THE TUSKEGEE AIRMEN: BREAKING BARRIERS IN THE SKY

> *"Excellence is a form of protest."*
>
> *- Wynton Marsalis*

Suppose one was being degraded for reasons unknown. In that case, showing what one can do is one of the best ways to counterattack. Tuskegee Airmen or any other person did not have to prove anything to anybody. Still, there was a necessity during their time. They fought for their places to fight for the country and for their places to fight racism.

- Over two years in aerial combat
- Training in Alabama, USA

RACISM AND DISCRIMINATION IN THE MILITARY

From the 1890s to the 1950s, segregation and the separation of Whites and African Americans were extreme in the United States of America. And during World War II, which broke out in 1938, the military was not an exemption. African Americans, who had it in them and wanted to serve the country in the military as volunteers, were faced with the same racism issue.

This era did not value the amount of patriotism and will a countryman has. No matter how strong these values were in the volunteers, most were not given the fighting roles.

Most ended up in the kitchen, cooking and serving food to military men or as laborers or repairmen. Their beds, recreational facilities, and dining halls were also segregated.

There was heavy prejudice towards African Americans, that they were not wise, skilled, brave, and worthy. Some publications stated these as facts, such as a 1925 Army War College false report that African Americans were unfit for any leading position, especially in aviation.

Civil rights organizations worked tirelessly to get the government to listen to their call for equality. Luckily, one of the issues, letting African Americans work in the aviation field, was soon addressed slightly positively.

African Americans who really pursued aviation to fly planes were trained privately. If not, they had to attend an all-Black school or institution offering these programs, such as the Civilian Pilot Training Program. They were banned in aviation schools attended by Whites.

If this discrimination happened in military schools and bases, just imagine what the bias was like for the rest of America.

Segregation in the US military limited the group's potential as a whole. Instead of unraveling the greatness in all the qualified volunteer fighters during critical times, the potential was swept under the rug.

Soon, training facilities were established for African Americans.

They were still segregated, but at the least, they were given a small platform to excel. One of the segregated training facilities built for African Americans was the Tuskegee Army Air Field. It is located in Alabama. It started operating in 1941.

The program was not spared from the bullying; it was initially judged and thought to fail.

"A waste of public funding," commented a White aviator. "It's just a matter of time. The program will fail."

It was then called an "experiment," an indication of a test that could proceed but was assumed to halt due to the trainees' prejudiced incompetence.

Due to the presumption being a mere experiment, the Tuskegee flight training for pilots and support personnel was given insufficient support. Funding was small, materials and equipment were old, and other necessities were provided at a limited number. These were in obvious contrast to bases attended by White trainees.

Doubt about the abilities of African Americans was widespread, not just among soldiers in the same military level position but also among those in higher positions, those most expected to have a leader-like attitude.

TRAINING AT TUSKEGEE: PREPARING FOR COMBAT

The Tuskegee Army Air Field became the go-to training site for African American students learning to fly combat planes, navigate air maps, drop bombs, and support air forces from the ground.

The Army Air Corps supervised this training site to see how good or bad African Americans could deliver tactical operations.

The Tuskegee flight training program was born from an agreement between the US military and the Tuskegee Institute, a historically Black college. The institute provided top-notch instructors, many of whom were Black aviators, engineers, and mechanics, who had excellent academic and practical standing in the field of national defense.

With the budget and resources cut and the critical conditions in which they would be trained for war, only the most qualified candidates were accepted into the Tuskegee program. The screening included high academic scores and rigid physical examinations. This eliminated chances for 60% of the cadet applicants, and thirteen cadets moved forward to the pilot training as part of the initial class.

Since the program was housed with great instructors, it was the bare minimum to have a curriculum that was really comprehensive and targeted. The curriculum design was sure to equip the trainees with high intellect, logic, and skills before fighting on the ground and in the air. The training was as strict as the training in the White bases. Although the aircraft distributed to the Tuskegee were outdated134, the instructors with incredible credibilities and skills had the know-how, skill over matter.

The cadets studied flight and ground instruction and incredibly detailed coursework. It included topics on meteorology, aircraft navigation, and aircraft mechanics. Intensive and contingent flight training or simulations in various aircraft also prepared the cadets for the rough routes, terrain, and fighting in the atmosphere. These were crucial to match, if not exceed, the tactics of European and Mediterranean threats.

The cadets' attention and attitude towards learning were superb. Soon, they mastered flying and maintaining crafts from PT-17 and PT-13 biplanes to advanced AT-6, AT-10, TB-25s, and P-47 trainers. The African American trainees' precision and accuracy wowed their instructors. They also showcased their camaraderie, leadership skills, and self-discipline.

In no time, the cadets were seen to be effectively

functional up in the air as they could already fly in combat formations and maneuvers. The cadets could move as if they were one, swiftly following commands.

While the instructors celebrated the proficiency of the cadets, the white officers supervising the Tuskegee pilots dismissed that fact. They went their own way to continue to give the African American pilots a hard time, such as refusing to fly with them.

"Oh, no," said one white officer, giggling. "We won't fly with any of them. They still had more to prove to get that level of support from us."

The highly challenging coursework of the program resulted in a decrease in the successful number of pilot graduates. Only five pilots made it out with flying colors in March 1942.

They were authorized to be second lieutenants in the US Army Air Forces and decorated with the Silver Wings Medals. They were the first African American military pilots in history.

OVERCOMING ADVERSITY: AIRMEN IN ACTION

The African American pilots did their best in whatever role they had to take.

Initially flying P-39 Airacobras and P-40 Warhawks, the cadets escorted bombardiers. They protected the bombers' critical formation. No matter how dismissive the white pilots and soldiers might be, they were extremely amazed by what the Tuskegee pilots showcased.

The Tuskegee pilots were assigned to the 99th Pursuit Squadron's early combat assignments in North Africa and Sicily. Their undeniable skill and expertise brought them to be integrated into the 332nd Fighter Group flying P-51 Mustangs.

"Oh, P-51 Mustang! You were my dream plane!" said one Tuskegee pilot as he excitedly ascended on the red-trailed military aircraft. "Let's get it on!"

Their aircraft were painted red on the tails. It was indeed easily recognized and marked by the enemies. The flyers of the red tails were the incredible ones.

Remember how the Tuskegee trainees were given

outdated airplanes for combat training? The Tuskegee trainees could fully master those airplanes' complex and complicated nature. Stepping into a modern aircraft like the P-51 Mustang made it easier for them. They adapted rather quickly and could fly as one with their red tails. They were able to navigate well under combative air.

One Allied bomber was on the verge of getting banished by one of the fastest enemy planes, the German Me-262 jet fighter. He quickly looked for a red tail.

"In red tails, we trust," the Allied bomber whispered, maneuvering under a red tail he just spotted.

One red tail, piloted by Captain Roscoe Brown, shot the German Me-262 jet fighter down.

The Allied bombers now had a bias; they wanted to be under the protection of the Red Tails, which was the trust the Tuskegee pilots earned from their White military comrades. On the other hand, the Axis fighters, the enemies, tried their best to move away from the Red Tails to lessen their chances of getting hit in their own territory. The Tuskegee Airmen hit over 300 enemy weapons and supplies, including aircraft, trains, tanks, and fuel depots.

The Tuskegee Air men's technical skills in going deep into high-risk areas to escort bombers were one of a kind.

Lower loss rates were recorded in the area protected by red tails than the other fighter crews. It was the displayed competence and reliability that made the bombers respect and seek the African American pilots.

But of course, the high-performance Tuskegee pilots also endured hits from the enemies. The African American women cared for the pilots' wounds and repaired the aircraft's wounds. This was one of the earliest showcases of gender inclusivity in military support.

The white men boxed the African Americans in judgment and hate that they never deserved. The African Americans were given little to no opportunities to improve their lives and learn more to contribute to society.

African Americans proved that the stereotypes they received from white men were trash.

"Charles Lindbergh would be proud of me," one Tuskegee pilot, who idolizes aviator Lindbergh, triumphantly whispered to his co-pilot.

"Congratulations, Red-Tailed Angel," his co-pilot responded, patting his back.

Were they celebrated by the civilians? Read on to know how they were seen outside the military dome.

LEGACY OF COURAGE: IMPACT AND RECOGNITION

Did the civilians know about their accomplishments? No. At least not yet. Despite their display of innovation and relevant contribution to the Allies, the Tuskegee Airmen were seldom covered in news presses during the war. The white pilots were always receiving the spotlight, and the African Americans' successes in their missions were given little air time or were set aside.

So, when? Were they ever recognized?

Life is tough, but sometimes, life surprises us with what we have been waiting for.

The time passed by, and the African Americans' significant contributions, such as the Tuskegee Airmen's prowess during the war, started to challenge the laws that were built to degrade their race. The brave and highly skilled heroes, the Tuskegee pilots, flew more than 15,000 sorties. With that, they earned 744 Air Medals, 150 Distinguished Flying Crosses, and several Bronze Stars and Purple Hearts.

This achievement was one of the facts that paved the way for the African Americans' call for equality. Eventually, in 1948, the US military erased segregation within their system. President Harry S. Truman signed Executive Order 9981, mandating equal treatment and equal opportunity in the military field.

In 2007, the unique military record of Tuskegee Airmen, which led to massive military reform in wartime, brought them to the stage of the US Congress to receive accolades and the highest honor, the Congressional Gold Medal.

The story and the symbols of the bravery and greatness of the Tuskegee Airmen are showcased in several museums. The Smithsonian Institution houses its Congressional Gold Medal today. The training field of the Tuskegee Airmen was also preserved and is now open for public visits.

Tuskegee Airmen Inc. held the legacy of these pilots alive by providing scholarships and education programs to aspiring aviators.

The Tuskegee Airmen's eagerness to fight for the nation took it further to fighting against segregation within the military. Their way was diplomatic and skills-based, a painful route full of discrimination that they had to endure. Reaching their defined and undefined goals by showcasing what they can do inspired broader civil rights activism.

KEY TAKEAWAY

Lesson Learned:

Words are powerful, and what we say, especially if we are seen as credible enough by a large audience, might stick and set the tone for an extended period. Like what the 1925 Army War College report stated about the African Americans being unfit for aviation roles and the segregation laws passed by the government, they did contribute to setting the discriminatory atmosphere in the American military and the rest of America. Publishing passages that are untrue, unsupported, and purely out of unreasonable hate and prejudice could destroy lives and dreams.

To shake and challenge the oppressive laws against African Americans, there had to be a move. The Tuskegee Airmen's move was to enter deep into the military and prove themselves that their race had something to offer and that everyone was wrong in putting them in the dark. Despite the limited resources provided to the cadets to hone their skills, they did not falter and even made it as the top airmen of their time.

If the government is compelling enough, it will not undermine the knowledge and strengths of any of its constituents. People of every race, gender, and age should be given proper treatment and equal opportunity to thrive.

Historical Fun Fact:

Bombers had no idea who their escorts were

Tuskegee pilots shot many German planes down, escorting Allied bombers. They didn't know that the pilots of the Red Tails were African Americans. When they learned about it, they were shocked.

Benjamin O. Davis Jr., Commanding officer to Major General in the US Air Force

During the Tuskegee Airmen's assignment as the 99th Pursuit Squadron, they were commanded by Benjamin O. Davis Jr., an African American. His determination and leadership skills were recognized, and soon, he became the first African American major general in the US Air Force.

ACTIVITY

Reflection Questions

1. Even after the Tuskegee cadets graduated, they still faced discrimination. Despite their precision and mastery during training, it took time before they were assigned to do frontline air duties. Do you agree that the Tuskegee Airmen shouldn't have let the White officers play tricks on them and that they should have retreated from piloting to try to frustrate the White officers for the wasted resources?

Yes/No

2. During the encounters, White bombers trusted the red tails for cover. Do you think it would have been better if the Tuskegee pilots pretended to accidentally shoot the white bombers to get revenge for the discrimination against African Americans?

Yes/No

8

THE BATTLE OF BRITAIN:
DEFENDING THE SKIES

> *"Victorious warriors win first and then go to war."*
>
> *- Sun Tzu*

Britain looked disadvantageous in the Battle of Britain due to limited resources and being outnumbered. But they had to defend the homeland, and securing the backline and frontline in order and ensuring good coordination contributed largely to their win.

- July 10 to October 31, 1940
- Skies of Britain

THE BLITZ BEGINS: BRITAIN UNDER SIEGE

Change of plans!

German military aircraft shifted their attacks from targeting the British military to targeting British cities.

It was the Blitz.

It was the first yet crippling phase of the Battle of Britain. Bombings in the cities were widespread.

The intense campaign to take down Britain's urban industry affected British morale.

Luckily, British people were resilient and quick to pick themselves up during the onslaught. Britain had developed remarkable innovations to help them in crucial times like this. They created a radar system called Chain Home. It effectively detected incoming enemy aircraft. Because of this innovation, the Royal Air Force, or RAF, was given ample time to prepare and intercept communication lines.

"This network of warning stations can spot and quickly disseminate information on any incoming foreign flyers," Air Chief Marshal Sir Hugh Dowding said.

"We have limited military resources, and the preparation time this Chain Home can buy us will be crucial in helping manage resources more effectively," one server officer nodded in agreement.

Bombings were continuous and destructive. Germany targeted London and neighboring cities. Civilians were under intense threat. They lived in hostile and uncertain situations. When sudden bombs fell, some civilians took cover under underground subways. These structures were sturdy enough to be temporary shelters, keeping lives. There was community spirit amidst the battle. People tried to help each other. More and more civilians could take refuge under engineered infrastructures in the cities.

Amidst the chaos, ordinary citizens found the courage to step up. Many joined civil defense organizations as air raid wardens. They patrolled neighborhoods to find possible rescues. They guided people to shelters and assisted with their immediate concerns. They also reported damage from the attacks.

The contributions of the ordinary citizens were invaluable in maintaining order in city communities. Their bravery gave inspiration to the community.

Some groups have innovated mobile setups for pantries and food counters. These initiatives sustained the communities' food and drinks. The Women's Voluntary Service, or WVS, was one of the key groups that took part in the drive to aid bombing victims who lost their homes. The mobile canteens also comforted the rescuers and wardens even under scary situations.

Another innovative defensive measure Britain pulled off was filling the sky over the cities with tethered barrage balloons. They did not always directly shoot German planes down. Still, they were pretty effective in shooing the enemies away to higher heights. When planes stay at altitudes higher than the recommended, the pilot will have difficulty targeting subjects.

The first encounters of the Battle of Britain were challenging. Still, the innovations and contributions from various system levels made the defense extra strong.

RAF VS LUFTWAFFE: AIR BATTLE FOR SURVIVAL

It was RAF versus the German Luftwaffe. The Germans were so eager to control the British skies first. Dowding commanded the RAF fighters. RAF's strategy was centralizing networks.

The information from the Chain Home, other radars, and the Observer Corps would be integrated into a robust central station. The Observer Corps involved over 30,000 human observers who signaled whenever enemy planes flew toward Britain at low altitudes. Especially because low-flying planes were mostly not within radar technology coverage. Their vigilance provided crucial tracking data, helping controllers vector fighters efficiently toward incoming raids.

The orderly and highly organized system, such as the establishing sector control rooms, enabled efficient and deep interception into German air formations.

The RAF focused on intercepting German bombers rather than engaging fighter escorts, a deliberate strategy to protect British infrastructure, preserve British strength, and target direct offense.

The RAF had two fighter planes, which served as the defense backbone. One was the agile Supermarine Spitfire, which was effective at dogfights, and the other was the sturdy Hawker Hurricane, which served as the first contact with incoming enemy bombers. These aircraft were modern and advanced, superior in their line. The Hurricane downed approximately 60% of enemy aircraft. The reliability of the weaponry was even more strengthened by its pilots' superb navigation and fighting skills. These posed challenging terrains for the German Luftwaffe.

The young RAF pilots were called "The Few" for the obvious reason of being outnumbered by the enemy. Their immense bravery and perseverance to face these facts in daily sorties was a good grade of patriotism. It was a determination that made them survive fighting for Britain.

Although the German Luftwaffe's primary goal was to control Britain's skies, the RAF still deployed ground crew to check, repair, and quickly make the damaged British aircraft ready and functional again.

A plane landed. The ground crew immediately checked on the RAF pilot. The pilot was bloody wounded.

"Captain-," the ground crew gave a hand sign to the medical crew to come over faster.

"Medical on the way," she told the captain while checking the plane's status.

"Cable frayed," the ground crew diagnosed.

"Can she still fly?" asked the pilot.

"Definitely, captain," the ground crew assured the pilot that the plane could recover. "Scratch-like issue."

The ground crew consisted of mechanics, engineers, and support personnel who equally served in the Battle of Britain, like the airmen.

TRIUMPH IN THE SKIES: BRITAIN'S VICTORY

Britain won the battle. It showed how maximizing resources, maintaining order, technological innovations, and executing impressive tactics could overcome being outnumbered.

With the determination of the people behind the warplanes, command centers, radar systems, and grounds, plus the leading actor, which was the advanced early warning system Chain Home, the British people were able to oust the Germans' evil intentions from the homeland. Despite being outnumbered, the fighters didn't back down, engaging the enemy. They refused to give up Britain to the enemies until the Germans were halted from achieving the air superiority they sought.

For 57 consecutive nights, cities across Britain endured relentless air raids. London bore the brunt of this assault, with the Germans dropping over 18,000 tons of bombs. Yet even as buildings crumbled and fires raged, the operations of essential services continued.

This "Blitz spirit" emerged from shared hardships. Families huddled in Underground stations while bombs fell overhead. Neighborhoods organized communal cooking when gas lines were damaged.

The RAF's ranks included 574 pilots from countries outside Britain. Polish squadrons achieved among the highest kill ratios, with their 303 Squadron downing 126 enemy aircraft. Czech, Canadian, and New Zealand pilots fought with exceptional ferocity, having witnessed firsthand what Nazi occupation meant for their homelands.

Air Chief Marshal Dowding also gained respect for managing the control system. His ability brought clarity and ensured great cross-coordination of RAF squadrons. With their sturdy and high-performing planes, fighters were efficiently directed to areas necessary to prevent the Germans from having the ball. The impact was massive enough to incur significant losses on the enemy.

Coastal Command also existed. It protected British shipping and attacked enemy vessels. Their long-range patrols identified and neutralized incoming threats. By disrupting German naval movements, they prevented seaborne reinforcement of air attacks.

Everyone's resilience, even those civilians and volunteers, kept the morale of the British people high overall. All fields were constantly under fire, yet the heart to fight for their homeland overpowered fear. The skill and attitude showcased by everyone who stepped up, went out of their comfort zones, and went beyond were paramount.

AFTERMATH AND SIGNIFICANCE OF THE BATTLE OF BRITAIN

Germany failed and could not risk an amphibious landing across the English Channel. Nazi's invincibility myth was now debunked.

Britain's successful defense significantly influenced American public opinion. The US soon supported the Allies. American involvement in the war was through increased material aid and, later, direct military participation.

Since Britain could maintain its sovereignty, Britain continued to serve as a base for Allied operations. This preserved platform was essential for the planning, staging, and execution of the eventual liberation of Western Europe, including the D-Day landings in 1944.

Women were praised for being great at their roles. They served in the Women's Auxiliary Air Force or WAAF. They operated radar stations, processed intelligence, and managed communications.

The conflict transformed air warfare doctrine. The success established principles that would influence military aviation for decades to come. It also introduced studies on advancing aircraft technology and tactics. Innovations in fighter design, radar systems, and aerial combat techniques influenced aviation development throughout the rest of the war and beyond.

The daytime air battles subsided after October 1940, but the Luftwaffe continued night bombing raids on British cities. Until Germany ultimately canceled Operation Sea Lion, the planned invasion of Britain through the seas.

The sacrifice of the Battle of Britain heroes are commemorated through annual ceremonies, memorials, museums, and publications.

KEY TAKEAWAY

Lesson Learned:

The Battle of Britain tells a lot about the importance of technology in the early years, especially in warfare. It will give one an advantage if one has the skills and knowledge to use and maximize advanced technology. In the Battle of Britain, it significantly increased Britain's chance to win in defense. There is enough reason to invest in researching and developing technologies that can help people's lives.

Keeping everything organized and coordinated reaps rewards. In a chaotic environment, striving for order matched with speed and critical thinking before raining bullets would allow efficiency and effectiveness to set in. Strategic management can overcome numerical disadvantages.

The story also underscored the decision-making and dedication of the support roles. The well-trained and brave crews on the ground, in server rooms, on observation decks, and even those taking care of the affected civilians emphasize that working together can withstand fear to some extent and give hope and inspiration in adversity.

Historical Fun Fact:

Use of dummy factories and aircraft

Britain placed dummy aircraft on airfields to leave the Germans thinking the fields were fortified. Dummy factories were also installed to keep enemies from attacking real ones. It was successful in diverting some attacks from the enemy.

Carrier Pigeons as backup

In wartime, contingency plans are a must. Although Britain had good communication technology during the battle, it did not rely solely on it. They sent messages and codes to other sectors through carrier pigeons.

ACTIVITY

Can you circle the correct answer?

1. The postponed naval mission of the German Luftwaffe against Britain was called Operation Sea Lion/ Operation North Sea.

2. Although the British military had technological radar systems, it still had human radars called Carrier Pigeons/ Observer Corps.

3. Two of the British Air Force's biggest assets were the Supermarine Spitfire and the Hawker Hurricane/ Hawker Chan.

4. Although many RAF pilots were British, the force also included pilots from 16 nations, including Poland, Czechoslovakia, Canada, and Japan/ New Zealand.

5. The daytime air battles subsided after October 1940/ October 1950.

6. The advanced early warning system detecting incoming German planes was called Radar Home/ Chain Home.

7. Britain deployed tethered hot air balloons/ barrage balloons to the sky to meddle with the German aerial formations.

Answers:

1. The postponed naval mission of the German Luftwaffe against Britain was called **Operation Sea Lion**.

2. Although the British military had technological radar systems, it still had human radars called **Observer Corps**.

3. Two of the British Air Force's biggest assets were the Supermarine Spitfire and the **Hawker Hurricane**.

4. Although many RAF pilots were British, the force also included pilots from 16 nations, including Poland, Czechoslovakia, Canada, and **New Zealand**.

5. The daytime air battles subsided after October 1940.

6. The advanced early warning system detecting incoming German planes was called **Chain Home**.

7. Britain deployed tethered **barrage balloons** to the sky to meddle with the German aerial formations.

9

THE WOMEN OF BLETCHLEY PARK:

CODEBREAKERS EXTRAORDINAIRE

> *"Women, like men, should try to do the impossible. And when they fail, their failure should be a challenge to others."*
>
> *– Amelia Earhart*

Cracking military codes seemed impossible, but it can be done with technology and human intelligence—women can. Humanity has to be proud of women's perseverance, as it leads to success if not continuous success.

- Codebreaking from 1939 to 1945
- Buckinghamshire, England

ENIGMA AND CODEBREAKING: BLETCHLEY'S SECRET WEAPON

Today's technology is impressive—but let's take a trip back to World War II to see the machine once thought unbreakable... until it was.

During World War II, Nazi Germany owned an Enigma machine that turned messages into codes. The codes were then sent around until they reached the intended receiver. The receiver would then decrypt to understand the message. This is crucial in safely sending the following steps, plans, changes, and strategies. Communication tampering was a thing in war, so these measures were present. Enigma was a typewriter-like device that used rotating wheels and a plugboard to scramble messages. The goal was for a code to be unbreakable or broken only by the person who intended to break it. With about 150 quintillion possible settings changed daily, Enigma made German communications appear impenetrable.

The Allies needed to double their work to keep up with German technology, so Britain built a network of codebreakers.

Bletchley Park, a facility in central England people would unlikely suspect of anything, became the center of Allied code-breaking efforts. The workforce included an unusual mix of linguists, mathematicians, chess players, crossword puzzle champions, teachers, typists, clerks, and telephone operators. They went onboarding without knowing what role they would really be taking. They didn't see the value they would bring to the national defense.

There were an estimated 10,000 codebreakers. These people were tasked with operating machines, managing operating machines, managing intelligence, and analyzing data.

There were also participants from various Allied nations. Polish mathematicians made early breakthroughs before the war. And, now, they were sharing their findings with the British intelligence group.

Alan Turing, a great mathematician, designed a codebreaker machine. It was called the "Bombe," a machine that automated their process. The Bombe could check over 20,000 possible Enigma settings per minute. That's the speed at which German codes are decrypted right there! This technology eventually allowed the team to regularly decrypt German messages.

At its peak, Bletchley Park staff decoded over 3,000 enemy communications about plans and movements daily.

One significant achievement was tracking U-boats, the German submarines that were sinking Allied supply ships. Once Enigma messages were decoded, Allied convoys could now avoid the submarines. Movement of vital supplies continued flowing from North America to Britain.

The tireless code-breaking at Bletchley Park influenced primary operations, including the D-Day landings, intercepting, and misleading German communication by directing enemy forces to faux landings. Historians estimate that World War II would have lasted two to four years without code-breaking.

The intelligent contributions of the women-dominated codebreakers and the technological innovations undeniably saved millions of lives.

Everyone at Bletchley Park signed the Official Secrets Act. In the act, they were prohibited from discussing their work. Many didn't tell their families what they did during the war. Many didn't talk about their roles for decades. In the year 1970, their contributions were finally declassified and celebrated.

WOMEN AT BLETCHLEY PARK: UNSUNG HEROES

Over 75% of Bletchley Park workers were women. That was two-thirds of the total number of people who worked clandestinely in the middle of Britain. These female codebreakers came from diverse backgrounds. Many were from ordinary backgrounds rather than elite institutions or schools. There were housewives and teenagers, too.

Also, many came from the Women's Royal Naval Service or WRNS, pronounced "Wrens." All the Bletchley Park codebreakers were selected for their intelligence, attention to detail, and discretion.

Women like Jean Valentine and Joan Clarke operated the complex Bombe and Colossus machines, devices requiring precise setup and monitoring.

"Are we that skilled to be entrusted with these machines with minimal training?" Jean whispered to herself.

"I guess we gotta train ourselves with these things!" Joan said as if she heard Jean's thoughts. They laughed.

Operators assigned to these machines became highly skilled technicians despite minimal technical training. They learned from their own navigation and little guidance.

Beyond manning machines, women filled crucial roles throughout the intelligence pipeline. Some women linguists translated decrypted German, Italian, or Japanese messages.

Others analyzed decoded data to spot likenesses in every round of messages. This was done to identify patterns in enemy communications or extract actionable intelligence.

The interpretations, submitted to the military decision board, allowed Allied forces to evade ambushes, protect convoys, and rescue prisoners of war.

These women at Bletchley Park worked long hours. There were tons of codes to decipher, and they had to work shifts to avoid wasting time. Their facilities in Bletchley Park were huts, often freezingly cold, with no heat technology. But they did not stop and kept operations running around the clock. The pressure was immense.

"The surroundings are telling me to stop," one codebreaker said while frequently breathing onto her hands for heat. "But how can I when delays can cost lives?"

They worked fast yet with absolute accuracy.

Despite their vital contributions, Bletchley Park women faced discrimination. Many received lesser pay than the men with equivalent responsibilities. Women also had limited opportunities to rise in rank. Another was that because of the nature of their work and the oath to keep silent about it, the achievements of these hardworking women remained unacknowledged for decades.

But whatever, this event was historical. It allowed women to participate in male-dominated fields such as science, technology, engineering, and mathematics. This wartime service opened doors to previously inaccessible or male-dominated careers.

The women of Bletchley Park broke the stigma. Women can do things the world thought only men can do. Women can take over complex technical and analytical work.

CRACKING THE CODE: INTELLIGENCE TRIUMPHS

The codebreakers were efficient, but it was not smooth sailing. The most significant barrier that they encountered was the naval version of Enigma. The codes used by Germans in the maritime force were more difficult than those of the army and air force. Its complexity included extra buttons, additional wheels, and specialized daily settings.

But soon, the women-dominated group of codebreakers made it. They penetrated the codes, proving that even more complex variants of the enemy technology were breakable when faced with skill and determination.

The Germans behind the radios didn't know that their conversations helped the codebreakers match codes with everyday phrases. They were studied, as well as their call behavior and speech.

"Please listen carefully and take notes," said the officer overseeing a group of codebreakers.

"I heard this a few times already," one codebreaker analyzed. They follow standard responses. They start and end with greetings."

These strict communication formatting led to pattern recognition by the Bletchley Park codebreakers. They got clues from it, which helped decode related messages.

The military collected all decrypted messages and classified them as ""ULTRA"" intelligence. Only the Allied commanders had access to the whole pile. Even the military leaders were refrained from receiving this intelligence. They were not even told where it came from. ULTRA was treated as highly confidential. Special security officers ensured ULTRA was passed around without any hint. The Germans must not suspect that their codes had been read.

The concealment happened so normally that the Germans didn't really suspect anything. And even after losing, they were more comfortable believing that Britain's success was a nod to good intelligence gathering, espionage, or luck, rather than thinking that their sturdy, reliable, and high-performing technology Enigma could have been heavily compromised and beaten.

Winston Churchill was concerned that decoding techniques could be used if other war approaches were exploited. The commitment of those involved to the secrecy of this mission was top-notch. The German forces never knew about it during those years.

Winston Churchill described the quietness and respect to the Official Secrets Act of the Bletchley Park codebreakers: the geese who laid the golden eggs and never cackled.

RECOGNITION AND LEGACY: WOMEN'S CONTRIBUTION TO HISTORY

After World War II, the women who secretly worked for the sake of defending the nation from Germans didn't get to enjoy the pride that they held. They didn't get to use these valuable experiences to find high-paying job positions.

They were still under oath to keep the secret role. Their Bletchley Park memories had become somewhat like only an imagination per se. But many decades later, in 1970, the secret was finally unraveling. The achievement of the women-dominated Bletchley Park operation was brought to public attention. Their hard work and intelligence were finally recognized.

Stories of Bletchley Park codebreakers filled news reports, books, documentaries, TV series like The Bletchley Circle, and films like The Imitation Game. The greatness of Jean Valentine, Joan Clarke, and Alan Turing was also revealed and admired by many. The respect and praise were long overdue, but it came. The story became instrumental in revisiting and understanding the horrors and the victories during World War II. It was a realization that no matter the background, women can do great things in a man's world. Another realization was that innovation in times of war is critical to work along with effective military engagements.

The stories of the women of Bletchley Park became monumental across generations. It inspired other women to pursue dreams in cybersecurity and other demanding careers. They were empowered and learned to believe their capabilities could go beyond what society had told them for a long time.

Institutions like schools, museums, and even Bletchley Park now dedicated time and space to narrate the stories of the women code breakers. This is to keep their legacy alive and be a source of inspiration, especially for young minds. This is to tell the world to keep going despite societal pressures. This also tells the world to keep learning and innovating things that save lives.

In 2009, surviving Bletchley Park veterans, including many women, were awarded a commemorative badge from the British government. They were secret weapons in service to the nation.

KEY TAKEAWAY

Lesson Learned:

The story of Bletchley Park illustrated how creativity can spark from the convergence of varied individuals. Solutions can emerge from anyone regardless of gender or background. The creation of technologies like the Bombe was a testament to this.

Intelligence and information are crucial during wartime. The handling of sensitive data can make or break a nation.

The admirable attitude exhibited by the Bletchley Park Codebreakers was profound. They showed commitment amidst time and societal pressures. They can't even talk about their roles; they can vent to no one after every stressful day.

The legacy of Bletchley Park marked intelligence, ingenuity, and the overlooked efforts and sacrifices individuals can make in shaping history. It is free to be kind and respectful. We'd never know who among us had served her life to live the life we get to live now.

Maintained Secrecy Outside the Workplace

Bletchley Park Codebreakers, although lodged at nearby hostels, of course, had families and friends outside work. There were times when they were asked about their work. To maintain critical secrecy, they just say they are engaged in "special work" or working at "Foreign Office".

Division of codes to Maintain secrecy

Some women Codebreakers never saw the whole message they were encrypting. It was like an individual or a small group was tasked with solving a small part of a bigger puzzle. This also contributed to keeping the ULTRA, in hindsight, away from enemy suspicion.

ACTIVITY

1. Where was Bletchley Park located?

2. How many percent of Bletchley Park codebreakers were women?

3. What Act bounded the Bletchley Park codebreakers' and the military to maintain secrecy in tasks and roles?

4. What did they call the codes that were successfully decoded?

5. The Allied naval ships were sinking, so the codebreakers intercepted German communication to learn about their movement. Were they successful in preventing the enemy from sinking Allied ships?

Answers:

1. Where was Bletchley Park located? **Center of England**

2. How many percent of Bletchley Park codebreakers were women? **75%**

3. What Act bounded the Bletchley Park codebreakers' and the military rule to maintain secrecy in tasks and roles? **Official Secrets Act**

4. What did they call the codes that were successfully decoded? **ULTRA**

5. The Allied naval ships were sinking, so the codebreakers intercepted German communication to learn about their movement. Were they successful in preventing the enemy from sinking Allied ships? **Yes, they prevented contact with German submarines which were sinking the Allied ships.**

PART THREE

IMPACT AND LEGACY

10

THE ATOMIC BOMBINGS OF HIROSHIMA AND NAGASAKI

> *"With knowledge comes power, and with power comes great responsibility."*
>
> *- Dianne Thompson*

Knowledge and power are the most sought-after combination. But both are two-edged swords. When used responsibly, they can better the world, but when used selfishly, they can destroy.

- Huge bombings on August 6 and August 9, 1945
- Hiroshima and Nagasaki, Japan

THE MANHATTAN PROJECT: RACE FOR THE ATOMIC BOMB

The Manhattan Project was America's secret mission to the first atomic bomb during World War II.

Would they make it? Will it be the first?

Fear drove the project's urgency. American leaders worried Hitler might develop nuclear weapons first.

The Manhattan Project brought together over 130,000 workers across multiple secret locations in the US. The locations included Los Alamos, New Mexico, Hanford, Washington, and Oak Ridge, Tennessee.

The workers were taken from the cream of the crop in physics, chemistry, and engineering. Some of these brilliant people were escapees from Nazi-occupied territories, giving them enough reason to participate in creating the grand weapon that would end the suffering and that would make the Axis forces regret their inhumane initiatives.

Most workers went to work daily without any idea what they were building. The government divided the work into smaller tasks and distributed them to different workers. Only a few scientists and military leaders knew the complete form of the parts worked on. Sounds familiar?

The previous chapter has the same treatment to task, the secrecy strategy at Bletchley Park.

Families of the atomic bomb workers also lived under strict security.

Richard Feynman, a physicist, was sending a letter to his wife.

A security officer asked, "Please," for the letter. Feynman handed it to him, and the officer read its contents.

"I'm sorry, officer. Why are you reading my mail?" Feynman said.

"Orders. I'm just making sure you're not in contact with anyone suspicious," the security personnel responded.

"I'm just letting my wife know I'm doing fine," Feynman said, sounding frustrated.

"Puzzle," the officer saw puzzle codes. "Puzzle codes for your wife?"

"I just wanted to give her something to think about," Feynman explained. "Maybe she'll forget about missing me."

"Please rewrite it. No codes," the security officer handed the letter back to Feynman.

Their mail exchanges were monitored, and they couldn't travel freely. These measures were executed to minimize the risk of data breaches and to control possible panic among US residents.

The US military and its allies worked at an extraordinary pace.

The cost was enormous. It almost reached $2 billion at the time. That is equivalent to about $36 billion today! And the energy consumption was also massive. It consumed 10% of all electricity produced in the US during the war years.

Yes, the US developed the first atomic bomb.

Germany surrendered in May 1945, so they were left with Japan. Japan was the last Axis force standing. The US now intended to use the bombs they were developing against Japan. Military leaders and President Harry S. Truman viewed the atomic bomb as a war-ender. They believed it was the quickest way to finally let Japan surrender. They also made estimates of casualties, and the computation resulted in one million Allied casualties if World War II did not end soon.

The rest of the advisors also wanted the war to end. However, the means didn't convince them. Many were not in favor of dropping an extremely dangerous and fatal bomb. But the decision to make use of the atomic bomb to target Japan won.

TARGETING HIROSHIMA AND NAGASAKI: DECISION AND DESTRUCTION

Great scientists like J. Robert Oppenheimer led the research and development of atomic bombs. They relied on fundamental scientific discoveries on nuclear subjects as the theoretical basis for their creation.

They worked really fast, and soon, the prototypes were ready.

"These will release unimaginable power," Oppenheimer predicted.

They conducted a test code-named "Trinity" in the desert of New Mexico. The explosion was so immense and impressive.

"Now I am become death, the destroyer of worlds", said Oppenheimer after witnessing the bomb's unimaginable power.

Soon, they were ready to take action.

They dropped the first atomic bomb from an American B-29 bomber called Enola Gay on Hiroshima. Hiroshima is a city complete with industrial buildings and even military facilities.

The first atomic bomb was uranium-based. It was named "Little Boy".

It was scary. The smoke, the deadly chemicals, and the rumbling of the grounds were widespread in the flat lands of Hiroshima. The estimate was that over 70,000 were killed by the impact. Survivors, or "hibakusha," suffered significant burn injuries from the blast and heat. Some developed radiation sickness.

Going back to the second atomic bomb drop, the original plan was to drop it at Kokura, Japan. Still, it didn't happen due to heavy clouds that condensed above it.

Instead, they dropped the second bomb on Nagasaki. This atomic bomb was plutonium-based and was code-named "Fat Man".

Nagasaki had bumpy, hilly terrain, which contained the effect of the bombing. Many buildings and other infrastructure had fallen, and approximately 40,000 people died from the immediate impact of the Fat Man. At the end of the year 1945, 30,000 survivors didn't make it because of excruciating pain, other diseases, and stress that the experience brought to their bodies and minds. Even thinking of what the future holds for them, given their depressed situation, they will be living a totally different life.

If the means were justified, the end is still being debated. While it ended a destructive war, the atomic bombs deployed killed thousands of innocent lives. Would weighing the number of casualties between whether or not nuclear bombs should be deployed matter? Because that was what the proponents were standing firm about.

With the encounters that passed, Japan had weakened its state and was moving towards raising the white flag even before the atomic bombings. However, the US only considered what was happening in real-time, and Japan still had not surrendered, continuing to be a threat to Allied forces. Rumors of peace talks were not given room.

The bombings happened on August 6 and 9, 1945, respectively. In August 1945, Japan surrendered. The official signing of surrender was the following month, marking the end of World War II.

AFTERMATH OF DEVASTATION: SURVIVORS AND FALLOUT

Hiroshima and Nagasaki were unrecognizable after the devastating bombings. Both cities were in rubble and ruins. Buildings were crushed like tin cans. The ground was a sea of fires snacking on the remains.

Rescuers found it extremely dangerous to dig into the scene because of persistent fire and radiation. Residents from other parts of Japan, not knowing the effects of being exposed to active chemicals from the bomb, also tried to search through the ruins for their families and friends. It was hard to tell between a living thing and a nonliving thing. Everything was in monochrome.

Many lives were instantly lost. Nearby hospitals were filled with injured and wrecked casualties. The revival was hampered by limited medical equipment, medicine, and health professionals to supply and service thousands. There were massive accounts of thermal burns, nausea, psychological stress, hair loss, and fatigue. Dust and rain were all contaminated with hazardous elements, which negatively affected the health of those exposed, humans, animals, and the environment. Some only survived for a few days to a few months. Those who managed through and lived longer had to live at risk of cancer. The tragic incident affected all ages, all genders, and all backgrounds.

Hiroshima and Nagasaki had become landscapes of grief. Efforts to rebuild the two painstakingly took many years. Survivors had to start rebuilding their lives from scratch. Despite the physical and emotional trauma, they had to move forward.

The health and demeanor of the survivors were monitored by medical personnel, and reports contributed to studies and efforts to understand and find a cure for cancer, at least to mitigate some of its symptoms and recurring effects.

The personal stories of survivors had been reminders of the catastrophe that The Manhattan Project caused. Their experiences led to global conferences on peace advocacy.

ETHICAL DEBATES AND LEGACY: IMPACT OF ATOMIC WARFARE

It was Albert Einstein and Leo Szilard, great scientists of the time, who informed President Roosevelt of the possibility of the Nazis developing nuclear weapons. They told the President how significant and destructive the impact could be. The letter from the scientists was written in 1939.

The US felt the rush, too terrified the Nazis were highly equipped to make this accurate. Therefore, they put up a plan to develop atomic bombs and hope to finish and launch ahead of the enemy.

The Manhattan Project and the final decision to launch the atomic bombs had raised concerns and debates across the globe.

It made those in the know uneasy before, during, and after the planned incident. It even made some scientists regret their participation and involvement. The worry that the unprecedented power of the bombs would kill many civilians became the ghost that would hunt them forever. The social problem revolved around the central issue of morality.

The Manhattan Project's secrecy level was also the talk of the town. There was the dilemma of keeping secrets for national security and safety, guarding from possible enemy breach, and letting the public know of the risks clung to dangerous projects, such as the atomic bombings of Hiroshima and Nagasaki.

The radioactive fallout from the Bombings extended its reach outside of Hiroshima and Nagasaki, affecting more and more lives for a more extended time.

The Manhattan Project could have ended World War II, but it gave birth to the Nuclear Age. Many saw the potential and started creating more destructive weapons. But this also was a transformative period in international relations. Although science and technology do wonders, the tragedy of Hiroshima and Nagasaki reminded them of the effects.

More studies emerged, and some scientists, such as Alan Robock, suggested that the thermonuclear war might end technological advancements and modernization. It was because nuclear emissions can also emit electromagnetic pulses that deter the functionality of mechanical subjects.

These scared people, especially people in power. Moreover, Mutual Assured Destruction, or MAD doctrine, was globally acknowledged. The idea was any nuclear attack-capable country that uses atomic weapons against another country with assumed same capabilities would only result in the annihilation of both. This way, nobody gets a reward. If you will get annihilated by harming another, and the other will get annihilated for retaliating, there would be no point in entering into a nuclear conflict. This doctrine will prevent atomic wars.

Museums in Japan housed memorabilia to remember and give tribute to the victims of atomic Bombings.

The story was also told in schools to instill in the young

minds the destruction hate can induce. Those wars must be prevented to prevent costly tragedies.

KEY TAKEAWAY

Lesson Learned:

The atomic bombings revealed destructive power unlike anything before. Its power was so far different from conventional arms that a doctrine had to be implemented to control future use. Many were killed by the atomic bombings of Hiroshima and Nagasaki. Countless others suffered from radiation afterward. These weren't just military strikes. The weaponry banished the entire cities in just a few snaps.

The tragedy showed why we must solve conflicts through diplomacy and peaceful means. Going violent, going nuclear is too devastating to accept.

These lessons remain relevant today as nations still possess thousands of nuclear weapons.

The secrecy of government and military projects must also be revisited, as many believe the public should be consulted on these matters, especially if their nature is fatal. The Manhattan Project itself taught hard lessons about freedom. Workers lived under constant surveillance, with censored mail and restricted travel.

Historical Fun Fact:

Cherry Trees Stood Still

Thirty Japanese cherry trees endured the devastating atomic bombing in Nagasaki. The trees stand close to ground zero, or the point where the bomb dropped. Until today, they stand firm with the help of tree surgeons.

Target Japanese areas that have no cultural significance

President Truman clearly stated not to bomb Japanese areas where culture was highly preserved. He stressed that the goal was to decapitate the Japanese military but not to destroy Japan's culture. He chose cities that had military facilities installed. The problem was these military facilities stood close to civilian homes.

ACTIVITY

1. Who were the two scientists who wrote about the possibility of the enemy developing nuclear weapons and the power of such?

2. Did the US successfully make the first atomic bomb?

3. Who was the President of the US when atomic bombings had to be decided upon?

4. What was the name of the project that created the first atomic bomb?

5. Where in Japan were Little Boy and Fat Man dropped?

6. Who was the scientist known for saying, "Now I am become death, the destroyer of worlds"?

Answers:

1. Who were the two scientists who wrote about the possibility of the enemy developing nuclear weapons and the power of such? **Albert Einstein and Leo Szilard**

2. Did the US successfully make the first atomic bomb? **Yes**

3.Who was the President of the US when atomic bombings had to be decided upon? **President Harry S. Truman**

4. What was the name of the project that created the first atomic bomb? **Manhattan Project**

5. Where in Japan were Little Boy and Fat Man dropped? **Hiroshima and Nagasaki**

6. Who was the scientist known for saying, "Now I am become death, the destroyer of worlds"? **J. Robert Oppenheimer, also known as Father of Atomic Bomb.**

REFERENCES

1. Struck, J. T. (2011). "The World Must Know What Happened, and Never Forget," Dwight David Eisenhower, Control of Masturbation, Missiles, Weapons, and the Holocaust - How Control of Difference in One Region Can Affect the Whole World. SSRN Electronic Journal. https://doi.org/10.2139/ssrn.1827246

2. PBS. (2025). World War II Major Events Timeline. Masterpiece. https://www.pbs.org/wgbh/masterpiece/specialfeatures/world-war-ii-major-events-timeline/#

3. Did the Soviet Union Invade Poland in September 1939? (n.d.). Msuweb.montclair.edu. https://msuweb.montclair.edu/~furrg/research/mlg09/did_ussr_invade_poland.html

4. A quote by Desmond Tutu. (n.d.). Www.goodreads.com. https://www.goodreads.com/quotes/5854748-my-humanity-is-bound-up-in-yours-for-we-can

5. Blitzkrieg explained. (n.d.). Imperial War Museums. https://www.iwm.org.uk/history/blitzkrieg-explained

6. Hughes, A, T., Royde-Smith, & Graham, J. (n.d.). World War II | Facts, summary, history, dates,

combatants, & Causes. Encyclopedia Britannica. https://www.britannica.com/event/World-War-II

7. Laurenceau, M. (2020, February 2). Bertram Ramsay - Commander-in-chief of the D-Day naval forces. D-Day Overlord.https://www.dday-overlord.com/en/battle-of-normandy/biographies/gb/bertram-ramsay#google_vignette

8. Battle of Dunkirk. (2025, March 7). History. https://www.history.com/articles/dunkirk

9. Webster, E. S. (2017, July 20). Dunkirk: What really happened. Teen Vogue. https://www.teenvogue.com/story/dunkirk-what-really-happened?utm

10. What you need to know about the Dunkirk evacuations. (n.d.). Imperial War Museums. https://www.iwm.org.uk/history/what-you-need-to-know-about-the-dunkirk-evacuations

11. Waxman, O. B., & Ronk, L. (2017, July 21). See harrowing footage of the real evacuation of Dunkirk in 1940. TIME. https://time.com/4864460/dunkirk-evacuation-photos/

12. Quinn, J. (2020, June 5). Miracles and Myths: The Dunkirk Evacuation – Part 3: Were the French abandoned at Dunkirk? - The National Archives blog. The National Archives Blog. https://blog.nationalarchives.gov.uk/

miracles-and-myths-the-dunkirk-evacuation-part-3-were-the-french-abandoned-at-dunkirk

13. [Crowe410]. (2017). British soldiers fire their rifles at German aircraft flying overhead during the evacuation of Dunkirk, May-June 1940 [1440×933] [Online forum post]. Reddit. https://www.reddit.com/r/HistoryPorn/comments/6ofm67/british_soldiers_fire_their_rifles_at_german/

14. Ramsgate's station history | RNLI. (2025). Rnli.org. https://rnli.org/find-my-nearest/lifeboat-stations/ramsgate-lifeboat-station/station-history-ramsgate

15. Davis, J. (n.d.). Western Front 1939-1940: The Little Ships. The Second World War. https://www.thesecondworldwar.org/western-front-1939-1940/operation-dynamo/the-little-ships

16. English Heritage. (n.d.). Operation Dynamo: Things you need to know about the Dunkirk Evacuation. https://www.english-heritage.org.uk/visit/places/dover-castle/history-and-stories/operation-dynamo-things-you-need-to-know/

17. The Editors of Encyclopaedia Britannica, Chmielewski, & Kenny. (n.d.). Timeline of the Dunkirk evacuation. Encyclopedia Britannica. https://www.britannica.com/story/timeline-of-the-dunkirk-evacuation

18. Pixelstorm. (2021, August 12). Fight them on the beaches. International Churchill Society. https://winstonchurchill.org/resources/speeches/1940-the-finest-hour/fight-them-on-the-beaches/

19. Dahlgreen, B. W. (2017, July 21). What actually happened at Dunkirk? https://www.bbc.com/news/entertainment-arts-40641801

20. Smith, R. (2017, July 10). Time Travel: Salvation at Dunkirk. HistoryNet. https://www.historynet.com/time-travel-salvation-dunkirk/

21. A quote from The Name of the Wind. (2025). Goodreads.com.https://www.goodreads.com/quotes/297928-the-day-we-fret-about-the-future-is-the-day

22. Anne Frank. (n.d.). Britannica Kids. https://kids.britannica.com/students/article/Anne-Frank/311323

23. Alpha History. (2012, July 24). Adolf Hitler's first address as chancellor (1933). Nazi Germany. https://alphahistory.com/nazigermany/hitlers-first-address-as-chancellor/

24. United States Holocaust Memorial Museum. (2021, August 3). Anne Frank: Biography. Ushmm.org; United States Holocaust Memorial Museum, Washington, DC. https://encyclopedia.ushmm.org/content/en/article/

anne-frank-biography

25. Just Another Kid: 10 Facts about Anne Frank | The Children's Museum of Indianapolis. (2021). Childrensmuseum.org. https://www.childrensmuseum.org/stories/10-facts-about-anne-frank

26. Biography: Anne Frank for Kids. (2004). Ducksters.com. https://www.ducksters.com/biography/women_leaders/anne_frank.php

27. Anne Frank House. (2019, April 15). Who Was Anne Frank? Anne Frank Website; Anne Frank House. https://www.annefrank.org/en/anne-frank/who-was-anne-frank/

28. Levy, D. S. (2017, May 12). How Anne Frank's Family Found a Place to Hide. TIME; Time. https://time.com/4770800/anne-frank-secret-annex

29. Margot Frank. (n.d.). Anne Frank Fonds. https://www.annefrank.ch/en/family/margot-frank

30. Anne Frank House. (2019, February 18). The Secret Annex. Anne Frank House. https://www.annefrank.org/en/anne-frank/secret-annex/

31. Website Filtered. (2025). Vogue.com. https://www.vogue.com/article/the-last-secret-of-the-secret-annex-essay

32. Anne Frank House. (2018, December 5). A typical day in the Secret Annex. Anne Frank Website. https://www.annefrank.org/en/anne-frank/go-in-depth/typical-day-secret-annex/

33. Anne Frank House. (2019, January 11). Anne Frank. Anne Frank Website. https://www.annefrank.org/en/

34. Remembering Anne Frank: a testament of courage and hope. (2024, April 30). So Dutchie. https://sodutchie.com/anne-frank-diary/

35. goodreads. (2018). Anne Frank Quotes (Author of The Diary of a Young Girl). Goodreads.com. https://www.goodreads.com/author/quotes/3720.Anne_Frank

36. Mercer, M. (2023). Honoring Anne Frank's Legacy. College of Arts & Sciences at Texas A&M University. https://liberalarts.tamu.edu/blog/2021/06/11/honoring-anne-franks-legacy/

37. Anne Frank at 90 – Schools Learn about Anne Frank's Life and Legacy. (2019). HWDSB. https://www.hwdsb.on.ca/blog/anne-frank-at-90-schools-learn-about-anne-franks-life-and-legacy/

38. How did Anne's diary become so famous? (n.d.). Anne Frank House. https://www.annefrank.org/en/anne-frank/diary/how-did-annes-diary-become-so-famous/

39. CORDER, M. (2024, October 16). A full-scale replica of Anne Frank's hidden annex is heading to New York for an exhibition. AP News. https://apnews.com/article/anne-frank-new-york-annex-diary-holocaust-8d093b71a48dcb84983a4ecf9d497747

40. Piccotti, T. (2022, June 9). Anne Frank - Diary, Quotes & Family. Biography. https://www.biography.com/authors-writers/anne-frank

41. Nast, C. (2018, May 2). Have You Heard of a Navajo Hogan? Architectural Digest. https://www.architecturaldigest.com/story/navajo-hogan-eco-friendly

42. Navajo sheep herding at risk from climate change. Some young people push to maintain the tradition. (2023, October 30). AP News. https://apnews.com/article/climate-change-drought-sheep-wool-navajo-shepherds-90de90e2fd59651d6a447ace5086076e

43. Hopkins, R. (2020, November 19). Native American Beadwork Is Inextricably Tied to Decolonization. Teen Vogue. https://teenvogue.com/story/native-american-beadwork-decolonization

44. Redsteer, M. H., Kelley, K. B., Francis, H., & Block, D. (2010). Increasing vulnerability to drought and climate change on the Navajo Nation: Observations of tribal elders, and an analysis of recent trends. U.S. Geological

Survey.https://www.preventionweb.net/english/hyogo/gar/2011/en/bgdocs/Redsteer_Kelley_Francis_&_Block_2010.pdf

45. Navajo Nation. (n.d.). Navajo culture. Discover Navajo. https://discovernavajo.com/navajo-culture/

46. Tsosie, R. (2007). Tribalism, constitutionalism, and cultural pluralism: Where do indigenous peoples fit within civil society? Tribal Law Journal, 8. University of New Mexico School of Law. https://digitalrepository.unm.edu/cgi/viewcontent.cgi?article=1071&context=tlj

47. Fiveable. (n.d.). Native American oral traditions & storytelling techniques. Fiveable. https://library.fiveable.me/american-literature-before-1860/unit-1/native-american-oral-traditions-storytelling-techniques/study-guide/vaHsu2Ideg1DLMIr

48. NavajoPeople.org. (n.d.). Navajo language. https://navajopeople.org/navajo-language.htm

49. Encyclopaedia Britannica. (n.d.). Navajo language. Britannica. https://www.britannica.com/topic/Navajo-language

50. Central Intelligence Agency. (2022, November 29). Navajo Code Talkers and the unbreakable code. https://www.cia.gov/stories/story/navajo-code-talkers-and-the-unbreakable-code/

51. Library of Congress. (n.d.). Navajo Code Talkers. https://guides.loc.gov/navajo-code-talkers

52. National Cryptologic Foundation. (n.d.). Native American Code Talkers. https://cryptologicfoundation.org/community/cryptologic-history/pioneers/native-american-code-talkers.html

53. Brownielocks. (n.d.). Navajo Code Talkers. https://www.brownielocks.com/navajocodetalkers.html

54. The National WWII Museum. (n.d.). American Indian Code Talkers. https://www.nationalww2museum.org/war/articles/american-indian-code-talkers

55. MacEachern, D. (2018, July 11). Navajo Code Talker facts: The unbreakable code. The Arizona Republic. https://www.azcentral.com/story/news/local/arizona/2018/07/11/navajo-code-talker-facts-unbreakable-code/460262002/

56. Vandenberg Space Force Base. (2007, November 8). Navajo Code Talkers: The code that was never broken. https://www.vandenberg.spaceforce.mil/News/Article-Display/Article/341248/navajo-code-talkers-the-code-that-was-never-broken/

57. Code talkers helped U.S. win World Wars I and II. (2024, February 13). U.S. Department of Defense. https://www.defense.gov/News/Feature-Stories/Story/

Article/3951611/code-talkers-helped-us-win-world-wars-i-and-ii/

58. National Museum of the American Indian. (n.d.). Recognition | Native words, Native warriors. https://americanindian.si.edu/nk360/code-talkers/recognition/

59. National Day Calendar. (n.d.). National Navajo Code Talkers Day – August 14. https://www.nationaldaycalendar.com/national-day/national-navajo-code-talkers-day-august-14

60. Google Arts & Culture. (n.d.). Native American Code Talkers – National Museum of the American Indian. https://artsandculture.google.com/story/native-american-code-talkers-national-museum-of-the-american-indian/yAXBAYZ9wwV7Jw?hl=en

61. Roberts, S. (2024, October 20). John Kinsel Sr., last of original Navajo Code Talkers, dies at 106. The New York Times. https://www.nytimes.com/2024/10/20/us/navajo-code-talker-john-kinsel-dead.html

62. GL Coverage. (2024, July 8). Quotes about defiance. https://glcoverage.com/2024/07/08/quotes-about-defiance/

63. Czech Ministry of Foreign Affairs. (1938). Munich Agreement. https://mzv.gov.cz/file/198473/MunichAgreement.pdf

64. Apple Podcasts. (n.d.). The Nazis: Road to War – Hitler Prepares to Strike (Part 1). https://podcasts.apple.com/no/podcast/the-nazis-road-to-war-hitler-prepares-to-strike-part-1/id1537788786?i=1000682836785&l=nb

65. Bleecker Street Media. (n.d.). Reinhard Heydrich: Anatomy of a monster. https://bleeckerstreetmedia.com/editorial/reinhard-heydrich-anatomy-of-a-monster

66. Operation Anthropoid, Tangmere and the assassination of Heydrich. (n.d.). Save Tangmere Tower. https://savetangmeretower.com/operation-anthropoid-tangmere-and-the-assassination-heydrich/

67. Jewish Virtual Library. (n.d.). Operation Anthropoid. https://www.jewishvirtuallibrary.org/operation-anthropoid

68. Warfare History Network. (n.d.). Operation Anthropoid: The planned killing of Reinhard Heydrich. https://warfarehistorynetwork.com/article/operation-anthropoid-the-planned-killing-of-reinhard-heydrich/

69. Radio Prague International. (2022, June 18). How the Sokol movement helped Operation Anthropoid succeed. https://english.radio.cz/how-sokol-movement-helped-operation-anthropoid-succeed-8751645

70. BBC News. (2016, August 2). Heydrich: The Nazi 'blond beast' whose assassination changed history.

https://www.bbc.com/news/world-europe-36944090

71. Woolf, N. (2016, August 3). The real story behind Anthropoid. Time. https://time.com/4439069/operation-anthropoid-historical-adviser

72. BBC Travel. (2017, August 31). A Prague church that defied Nazi rule. https://www.bbc.com/travel/article/20170831-a-prague-church-that-defied-nazi-rule

73. Cairns, D. (2017, June 13). Heydrich! Heydrich! Heydrich! Heydrich!. https://dcairns.wordpress.com/2017/06/13/heydrich-heydrich-heydrich-heydrich/

74. Kakutani, M. (2012, January 6). Review: Books about Heinrich Himmler and Reinhard Heydrich. The New York Times. https://www.nytimes.com/2012/01/08/books/review/books-about-heinrich-himmler-and-reinhard-heydrich-review.html

75. Touring Auschwitz. (n.d.). Top 10 movies on Reinhard Heydrich. https://www.touringauschwitz.com/post/top-10-movies-on-reinhard-heydrich

76. MacDonald, C. (2009). The assassination of Reinhard Heydrich. Birlinn. https://www.amazon.com/Assassination-Reinhard-Heydrich-Callum-MacDonald/dp/1843410362

77. Find a Grave. (n.d.). Karel Čurda. https://www.

findagrave.com/memorial/66910128/karel-curda

78. Murphy Jr., B. (2024). 365 inspirational quotes for 2025. Inc. https://www.inc.com/bill-murphy-jr/365-inspirational-quotes-for-2025/91066225

79. The Holocaust Explained. (n.d.). Conditions inside the Warsaw Ghetto. https://www.theholocaustexplained.org/the-camps/the-warsaw-ghetto-a-case-study/conditions-inside-the-warsaw-ghetto/

80. Imperial War Museums. (n.d.). Daily life in the Warsaw Ghetto. https://www.iwm.org.uk/history/daily-life-in-the-warsaw-ghetto

81. Facing History & Ourselves. (n.d.). Warsaw Ghetto Uprising. https://facinghistory.org/resource-library/warsaw-ghetto-uprising?

82. European Network Remembrance and Solidarity. (n.d.). Childhood and education lost in the ghettos. https://enrs.eu/news/childhood-and-education-lost-in-the-ghettos

83. United States Holocaust Memorial Museum. (n.d.). Spiritual resistance in the ghettos. https://encyclopedia.ushmm.org/content/en/article/spiritual-resistance-in-the-ghettos

84. Deportations from Warsaw Ghetto to Treblinka

begin. (n.d.). History.com. https://www.history.com/this-day-in-history/july-22/deportations-from-warsaw-ghetto-to-treblinka-begin

85. Jewish Historical Institute. (n.d.). July 28, 1942: Establishment of the Jewish Combat Organization. https://www.jhi.pl/en/articles/july-28-1942-establishment-of-the-jewish-combat-organization%2C693

86. Wired. (2008, April 25). WWII Jewish insurgents remembered for Warsaw ghetto uprising. https://www.wired.com/2008/04/wwii-jewish-ins/

87. Yad Vashem. (n.d.). Resistance in the Warsaw Ghetto. https://www.yadvashem.org/education/educational-materials/online-exhibitions/warsaw-ghetto-uprising/resistance.html

88. The Holocaust Explained. (n.d.). The Warsaw Ghetto Uprising. https://www.theholocaustexplained.org/resistance-and-rescue/jewish-resistance/the-warsaw-ghetto-uprising/

89. Jewish Women's Archive. (n.d.). Anilewicz, Mordecai. https://jwa.org/encyclopedia/article/anilewicz-mordecai

90. United States Holocaust Memorial Museum. (n.d.). Jewish women in the ghettos and camps. https://encyclopedia.ushmm.org/content/en/article/jewish-

-women-in-the-ghettos-and-camps

91. PolandWW2.com. (n.d.). Search results: WarsawGhetto.https://www.polandww2.com/?s=warsaw+ghetto

92. Facing History & Ourselves. (n.d.). Organizing resistance in the Warsaw Ghetto. https://www.facinghistory.org/holocaust-and-human-behavior/warsaw-ghetto-uprising/organizing-resistance

93. United States Holocaust Memorial Museum. (n.d.). Warsaw Ghetto Uprising. https://www.ushmm.org/learn/holocaust/ghettos/warsaw/warsaw-ghetto-uprising

94. United States Holocaust Memorial Museum. (n.d.). Warsaw Ghetto Uprising. https://encyclopedia.ushmm.org/content/en/article/warsaw-ghetto-uprising

95. Jewish Virtual Library. (n.d.). The Warsaw Ghetto Uprising.https://www.jewishvirtuallibrary.org/the-warsaw-ghetto-uprising

96. The Holocaust Explained. (n.d.). The Warsaw Ghetto Uprising. https://www.theholocaustexplained.org/resistance-and-rescue/jewish-resistance/the-warsaw-ghetto-uprising/

97. Jewish Virtual Library. (n.d.). Mila 18. https://www.

.jewishvirtuallibrary.org/mila-18

98. UNESCO. (n.d.). Jürgen Stroop's report on the Warsaw Ghetto Uprising. https://www.unesco.org/en/memory-world/jurgen-stroops-report

99. Museum of Jewish Heritage. (n.d.). Ada Feingold's eyewitness account of the Warsaw Ghetto Uprising. https://mjhnyc.org/blog/ada-feingolds-eyewitness-account-of-the-warsaw-ghetto-uprising/

100. United States Holocaust Memorial Museum. (n.d.). Jewish uprisings in ghettos and camps, 1941–44. https://encyclopedia.ushmm.org/content/en/article/jewish-uprisings-in-ghettos-and-camps-1941-44

101. Jewish Heritage Europe. (2024, April 19). Poland: Warsaw Ghetto memory. https://jewish-heritage-europe.eu/2024/04/19/poland-ghetto

102. Latson, J. (2017, April 20). This is what it was like to survive the Warsaw Ghetto. Time. https://time.com/4779148/warsaw-ghetto-survivor-account/

103. POLIN Museum of the History of Polish Jews. (2023, January 16). Unique discovery: Photographic film with images of Warsaw Ghetto Uprising. https://polin.pl/en/news/2023/01/16/unique-discovery-photographic-film-images-warsaw-ghetto-uprising

104. AFS India. (2018, July 11). Empathy is about finding echoes of another person in yourself. https://india.afs.org/2018/07/11/empathy-is-about-finding-echoes-of-another-person-in-yourself

105. United States Holocaust Memorial Museum. (n.d.). Introduction to the Holocaust. https://encyclopedia.ushmm.org/content/en/article/introduction-to-the-holocaust

106. Imperial War Museums. (n.d.). What was Kristallnacht? https://www.iwm.org.uk/history/what-was-kristallnacht

107. Imperial War Museums. (n.d.). What was the Holocaust? https://www.iwm.org.uk/history/what-was-the-holocaust

108. Museum of Jewish Heritage. (n.d.). The forgotten life of Herschel Grynszpan. https://mjhnyc.org/blog/the-forgotten-life-of-herschel-grynszpan/

109. Kindertransport Association. (n.d.). The organisers of Kindertransport. https://kindertransport.org/history/the-organisers/

110. The National Archives (UK). (n.d.). Kindertransport. https://www.nationalarchives.gov.uk/education/resources/kindertransport/

111. Jewish Virtual Library. (n.d.). The Kindertransport. https://www.jewishvirtuallibrary.org/the-kindertransport

112. Kindertransport Association. (2019). Kindertransport 2019. https://kindertransport.org/2019

113. The Wiener Holocaust Library. (n.d.). Search results: Kindertransport. https://wienerholocaustlibrary.org/?s=kindertransport

114. Nicholas Winton Foundation. (n.d.). Kindertransport exhibition. https://nicholaswinton.com/exhibition/kindertransport

115. Aish.com. (n.d.). How a Kindertransport saved and shaped my mother-in-law's life. https://aish.com/how-a-kindertransport-saved-and-shaped-my-mother-in-laws-life-2/

116. Bradshaw, P. (2000, November 17). Nicholas Winton and Kindertransport: A life remembered. The Guardian. https://theguardian.com/film/2000/nov/17/culture.features2

117. UCL Press. (n.d.). Kindertransport: Memory, identity and the Holocaust. https://journals.uclpress.co.uk/jhs/article/id/1287/print/

118. New York University. (2016, December).

Kindertransport: Rescuing children on the brink of war. https://www.nyu.edu/about/news-publications/news/2016/december/Kindertransport.html

119. History Skills. (n.d.). Kindertransport. https://www.historyskills.com/classroom/year-10/kindertransport/

120. Kindertransport Memorial. (n.d.). Kindertransport memorial. https://kindertransport-memorial.org/

121. King, A. (n.d.). The Kindertransport sculptures of Frank Meisler. https://www.andrewkingphotography.co.uk/the-kindertransport-sculptures-of-frank-meisler-2/

122. Holocaust Memorial Day Trust. (n.d.). Secondary Kindertransport lesson plan. https://hmd.org.uk/resource/secondary-kindertransport-lesson-plan/

123. Europeana. (n.d.). The Kindertransport. https://www.europeana.eu/en/stories/the-kindertransport

124. Yad Vashem. (n.d.). Nicholas Winton. https://www.yadvashem.org/holocaust/stories/nicholas-winton.html

125. The Guardian. (2023, December 7). How Nicholas Winton saved 669 children—and counting—from the Holocaust: He became everybody's grandfather.

https://www.theguardian.com/lifeandstyle/2023/dec/07/how-nicholas-winton-saved-669-children-and-counting-from-the-holocaust-he-became-everybodys-grandfather

126. Marsalis, W. (n.d.). Excellence is a form of protest. https://wyntonmarsalis.org/news/entry/excellence-is-a-form-of-protest-wynton-marsalis

127. The National WWII Museum. (n.d.). Race and racism in World War II. https://www.nationalww2museum.org/students-teachers/student-resources/race-and-racism-world-war-ii

128. CAF Rise Above. (n.d.). The 1925 Army War College report. https://cafriseabove.org/the-1925-army-war-college-report/

129. Franklin D. Roosevelt Presidential Library and Museum. (n.d.). Tuskegee. https://www.fdrlibrary.org/tuskegee

130. MIT Black History. (n.d.). Tuskegee Airmen. https://www.blackhistory.mit.edu/story/tuskegee-airmen

131. National Park Service. (n.d.). Tuskegee Airmen: Airprint. https://www.nps.gov/museum/exhibits/tuskegee/airprint.htm

132. Tuskegee University. (n.d.). Tuskegee Airmen facts. https://www.tuskegee.edu/support-tu/tuskegee-airmen/tuskegee-airmen-facts

133. Tuskegee Airmen Inc. (2014). Tuskegee Airmen: Questions and answers. https://tuskegeeairmen.org/wp-content/uploads/2020/11/TAI_Resources_Tuskegee-Airmen-Questions-and-Answers-09_2014.pdf

134. Tuskegee Airmen National Museum. (n.d.). Aircraft history. https://tuskegeemuseum.org/aircraft-history/

135. Smithsonian National Air and Space Museum. (n.d.). Tuskegee Airmen. https://airandspace.si.edu/explore/stories/tuskegee-airmen

136. U.S. Air Force. (n.d.). Training at Tuskegee: Turning dreams into reality. https://www.af.mil/News/Article-Display/Article/473258/training-at-tuskegee-turning-dreams-into-reality/

137. Tuskegee Airmen Inc. (n.d.). The people. https://tuskegeeairmen.org/legacy/the-people/

138. 15th Air Force. (n.d.). 332nd Fighter Group. https://15thaf.org/XV%20FC/306th%20FW/332nd%20FG/default.html

139. U.S. Department of Veterans Affairs. (n.d.). The

Tuskegee Airmen: 332nd Fighter Group's Red Tails. https://news.va.gov/130142/the-tuskegee-airmen-332nd-fighter-groups-red-tails/

140. Captain Roscoe Brown. (n.d.). The National WWII Museum. https://www.nationalww2museum.org/war/articles/captain-roscoe-brown

141. National Association of Black Military Women. (n.d.). Women of Tuskegee. https://www.nabmw.org/women-of-tuskegee

142. The National WWII Museum. (n.d.). Tuskegee Airmen: Interview with Daniel Haulman. https://www.nationalww2museum.org/war/articles/tuskegee-airmen-interview-daniel-haulman

143. San Diego Air & Space Museum. (n.d.). Tuskegee Airmen. https://sandiegoairandspace.org/hall-of-fame/honoree/tuskegee-airmen

144. Library of Congress. (n.d.). Equality of treatment and opportunity. https://www.loc.gov/collections/veterans-history-project-collection/serving-our-voices/diverse-experiences-in-service/equality-of-treatment-and-opportunity/

145. National Park Service. (n.d.). The Tuskegee Airmen: Training and stateside experiences. https://www.nps.gov/articles/000/the-tuskegee-airmen-training-and-

stateside-experiences-teaching-with-historic-places.htm

146. Tuskegee Airmen Inc. (n.d.). Tuskegee Airmen Scholarship Foundation. https://tuskegeeairmen.org/youth/tuskegee-airmen-scholarship-foundation/

147. Losey, S. (2017, May 21). Red Tails reunited: Pioneering Tuskegee Airmen proudly look back. Air Force Times. https://www.airforcetimes.com/news/your-air-force/2017/05/21/red-tails-reunited-pioneering-tuskegee-airmen-proudly-look-back/

148. Encyclopædia Britannica. (n.d.). Benjamin O. Davis Jr.. https://www.britannica.com/biography/Benjamin-O-Davis-Jr

149. BrainyQuote. (n.d.). Sun Tzu: Victorious warriors win first and then go to war.... https://www.brainyquote.com/quotes/sun_tzu_387509

150. Morale. (n.d.). Leeds Beckett University. https://www.leedsbeckett.ac.uk/school-of-humanities-and-social-sciences/leeds-blitz/morale/

151. Imperial War Museums. (n.d.). How radar changed the Second World War. https://www.iwm.org.uk/history/how-radar-changed-the-second-world-war

152. Imperial War Museums. (n.d.). Life in the

Anderson shelter. https://www.iwm.org.uk/history/life-in-the-anderson-shelter

153. The National Archives. (n.d.). Air raid precautions. https://www.nationalarchives.gov.uk/education/resources/second-world-war/air-raid-precautions/

154. The WVS at war. (n.d.). Imperial War Museums. https://www.iwm.org.uk/history/the-wvs-at-war

155. Barrage balloons. (n.d.). Royal Air Force Museum. https://www.rafmuseum.org.uk/research/online-exhibitions/history-of-the-raf/1939-1945-the-second-world-war/the-battle-of-britain/barrage-balloons.aspx

156. Hugh Dowding. (n.d.). Royal Air Force Museum. https://www.rafmuseum.org.uk/research/online-exhibitions/history-of-the-raf/people-of-the-raf/hugh-dowding.aspx

157. The Royal Observer Corps. (n.d.). Air & Space Magazine. https://www.airspacemag.com/military-aviation/the-royal-observer-corps-180975708/

158. Support from the ground in the Battle of Britain. (n.d.). Imperial War Museums. https://www.iwm.org.uk/history/support-from-the-ground-in-the-battle-of-britain

159. German air attacks. (n.d.). The National Archives.

https://www.nationalarchives.gov.uk/education/resources/home-front-1939-1945-part-one/german-air-attacks/

160. How the Luftwaffe fought the Battle of Britain. (n.d.). Imperial War Museums. https://www.iwm.org.uk/history/how-the-luftwaffe-fought-the-battle-of-britain

161. Never in the field of human conflict. (n.d.). Imperial War Museums. https://www.iwm.org.uk/visits/churchill-war-rooms/history-and-stories/never-in-the-field-of-human-conflict

162. Archive story. (n.d.). University of Iowa. https://magazine.foriowa.org/archive/archive-story.php?ed=true&storyid=1207

163. The Blitz begins. (n.d.). BBC. https://www.bbc.co.uk/history/ww2peopleswar/stories/06/a2765006.shtml

164. The Blitz begins. (n.d.). History.com. https://www.history.com/this-day-in-history/the-blitz-begins

165. The Blitz. (n.d.). Historic UK. https://www.historic-uk.com/HistoryUK/HistoryofBritain/The-Blitz/

166. The Polish pilots in the Battle of Britain. (n.d.). Imperial War Museums. https://www.iwm.org.uk/history/the-polish-pilots-in-the-battle-of-britain

167. How Britain won the Battle of Britain. (n.d.). Air & Space Magazine. https://www.airspacemag.com/history-of-flight/how-britain-won-battle-britain-180976088/

168. The unsung heroes. (n.d.). Battle of Britain Memorial. https://www.battleofbritain.net/the-unsung-heroes/

169. The Battle of Britain: Strategic impact on air warfare. (n.d.). Fly a Jet Fighter. https://www.flyajetfighter.com/the-battle-of-britain-strategic-impact-on-air-warfare/

170. Operation Sea Lion: Hitler's cancelled invasion of Britain. (n.d.). Warfare History Network. https://warfarehistorynetwork.com/article/operation-sea-lion-hitlers-cancelled-invasion-of-britain/

171. Battle of Britain: Celebrating and commemorating the Few, 75 years later. (2015, September 15). GOV.UK. https://www.gov.uk/government/speeches/battle-of-britain-celebrating-and-commemorating-the-few-75-years-later

172. Britain. (n.d.). Sunny CV. http://sunnycv.com/steve/WW2Timeline/britain.html

173. WWII carrier pigeon finally delivers secret message. (2012, November 15). ABC News. http://abcnews.go.com/blogs/headlines/2012/11/wwii-carrier-

pigeon-finally-delivers-secret-message

174. Women empowerment quotes. (n.d.). TeamBuilding. https://teambuilding.com/blog/women-empowerment-quotes

175. Enigma machine. (n.d.). National Security Agency. https://www.nsa.gov/cybersecurity-missions/cybersecurity-national-mission/protect-national-security-systems/historical-corner/enigma-machine/

176. How breaking Enigma helped win World War Two. (n.d.). Imperial War Museums. https://www.iwm.org.uk/history/how-breaking-enigma-helped-win-world-war-two

177. What was Bletchley Park? (n.d.). Bletchley Park. https://bletchleypark.org.uk/what-was-bletchley-park/

178. Marian Rejewski. (n.d.). Central Intelligence Agency.https://www.cia.gov/stories/story/marian-rejewski/

179. Codebreaking: Alan Turing and the Enigma machine. (n.d.). The National WWII Museum. https://www.nationalww2museum.org/war/articles/codebreaking-alan-turing-and-enigma-machine

180. What happened at Bletchley Park? (n.d.). Bletchley Park. https://bletchleypark.org.uk/learn/what-

happened-at-bletchley-park

181. The Enigma machine. (n.d.). Imperial War Museums. https://www.iwm.org.uk/history/the-enigma-machine

182. Enigma. (n.d.). BBC. https://www.bbc.co.uk/history/worldwars/wwtwo/enigma_01.shtml

183. Codebreaking and ciphers in the Second World War. (n.d.). The British Library. https://www.bl.uk/world-war-one/articles/codebreaking-and-ciphers-in-the-second-world-war

184. Women codebreaking in the Second World War. (2021, March 8). The National Archives Blog. https://blog.nationalarchives.gov.uk/women-codebreaking-second-world-war/

185. Jean Valentine: A Wren at Bletchley Park. (n.d.). Imperial War Museums. https://www.iwm.org.uk/history/jean-valentine-a-wren-at-bletchley-park

186. Colossus. (n.d.). Science Museum. https://www.sciencemuseum.org.uk/objects-and-stories/computing/colossus

187. Women codebreaking in the Second World War. (2021, March 8). The National Archives Blog. https://blog.nationalarchives.gov.uk/women-codebreaking-second-

-world-war/

188. Our story. (n.d.). Bletchley Park. https://bletchleypark.org.uk/our-story

189. The secret life of Bletchley Park's women. (n.d.). Smithsonian Magazine. https://www.smithsonianmag.com/history/secret-life-bletchley-park-women-180975441/

190. Cracking the Enigma code. (n.d.). The National WWII Museum. https://www.nationalww2museum.org/war/articles/cracking-enigma-code

191. [Author not specified]. (n.d.). [Title not specified]. ProQuest. https://www.proquest.com/docview/213083681?sourcetype=Scholarly%20Journals

192. Bletchley Park's secret war. (2015, September 13). CNN. https://www.cnn.com/2015/09/13/europe/bletchley-secret-war/index.html

193. Women in WWII. (n.d.). The National WWII Museum. https://www.nationalww2museum.org/students-teachers/student-resources/research-starters/women-wwii

194. WW2 and the Cold War. (n.d.). MI5. https://www.mi5.gov.uk/ww2-and-the-cold-war

195. The Bletchley Circle. (n.d.). PBS. https://www.

pbs.org/program/bletchley-circle/

196. Women codebreakers celebrated. (2018, June 22). The National Museum of Computing. https://www.tnmoc.org/news-releases/2018/6/22/women-codebreakers-celebrated

197. Secondary curriculum: Key stage 3 and 4. (n.d.). GOV.UK. https://www.gov.uk/government/publications/secondary-curriculum-key-stage-3-and-4

198. Code-breakers honoured for their secret service. (2009, July 14). The Telegraph. https://www.telegraph.co.uk/news/uknews/defence/5828410/Code-breakers-honoured-for-their-secret-service.html

199. War of secrets: Cryptology in WWII. (n.d.). National Museum of the U.S. Air Force. https://www.nationalmuseum.af.mil/Visit/Museum-Exhibits/Fact-Sheets/Display/Article/196193/war-of-secrets-cryptology-in-wwii/

200. With knowledge comes power—and with power comes great responsibility. (2011, July 21). Research Live. https://www.research-live.com/article/news/with-knowledge-comes-power-and-with-power-comes-great-responsibility/id/4011410

201. Atomic Heritage Foundation. (n.d.). https://www.atomicheritage.org

202. Manhattan Project history. (n.d.). Los Alamos National Laboratory. https://www.lanl.gov/discover/history/manhattan-project.php

203. Manhattan Project. (n.d.). U.S. Department of Energy. https://www.energy.gov/manhattan-project

204. Oppenheimer: Atomic secrets. (n.d.). PBS American Experience. https://www.pbs.org/wgbh/americanexperience/features/oppenheimer-atomic-secrets/

205. Security and secrecy. (n.d.). Atomic Heritage Foundation. https://ahf.nuclearmuseum.org/ahf/history/security-and-secrecy/

206. Making the atomic bomb: Trinity test. (n.d.). The National WWII Museum. https://www.nationalww2museum.org/war/articles/making-the-atomic-bomb-trinity-test

207. World War II primary resources. (n.d.). MacArthur Memorial Education Programs. https://macarthurmemorial.org/DocumentCenter/View/438/World-War-II-Education-Resources

208. Decision to drop the atomic bomb. (n.d.). Harry S. Truman Library & Museum. https://www.trumanlibrary.gov/education/presidential-inquiries/decision-drop-atomic-bomb

209. Japan was already defeated: The case against the nuclear bomb—and for basic morality. (n.d.). American Enterprise Institute. https://www.aei.org/op-eds/japan-was-already-defeated-the-case-against-the-nuclear-bomb-and-for-basic-morality/

210. Trinity Site. (n.d.). National Park Service. https://www.nps.gov/trinity/index.htm

211. The Manhattan Project: Robert Oppenheimer. (n.d.). Wired. https://www.wired.com/story/manhattan-project-robert-oppenheimer/

212. Hiroshima and Nagasaki. (n.d.). Atomic Heritage Foundation. https://www.atomicheritage.org/history/hiroshima-and-nagasaki

213. Statistics. (n.d.). Manhattan Project Voices. https://manhattanprojectvoices.org/oral-histories/statistics

214. Truman: Hiroshima. (n.d.). PBS American Experience. https://www.pbs.org/wgbh/americanexperience/features/truman-hiroshima/

215. After the bomb. (n.d.). Time. https://time.com/after-the-bomb/

216. [Author not specified]. (n.d.). [Title not specified]. PubMed Central. https://pmc.ncbi.nlm.nih.gov/articles/

PMC4990102/

217. Hiroshima and Nagasaki bombings. (n.d.). International Campaign to Abolish Nuclear Weapons. https://www.icanw.org/hiroshima_and_nagasaki_bombings

218. Einstein–Szilárd letter. (n.d.). Atomic Heritage Foundation. https://ahf.nuclearmuseum.org/ahf/key-documents/einstein-szilard-letter/

219. The Manhattan Project: The race to build the atomic bomb. (n.d.). Bulletin of the Atomic Scientists. https://thebulletin.org/virtual-tour/the-manhattan-project-the-race-to-build-the-atomic-bomb/

220. Manhattan Project National Historical Park. (n.d.). National Park Service. https://www.nps.gov/mapr/learn/manhattan-project.htm

221. Oppenheimer sheds new light on the legacies of the Manhattan Project: Nuclear legacy, public health hazards, and governmental secrecy. (2023, August 3). The Economic Times. https://m.economictimes.com/news/new-updates/oppenheimer-sheds-new-light-on-the-legacies-of-the-manhattan-project-nuclear-legacy-public-health-hazards-and-governmental-secrecy/articleshow/102378394.cms

222. Nuclear war would cause global famine and

kill billions, Rutgers-led study finds. (n.d.). Rutgers University. https://www.rutgers.edu/news/nuclear-war-would-cause-global-famine-and-kill-billions-rutgers-led-study-finds

223. Managing the Cold War 1962-85: Danger of Mutually Assured Destruction. (n.d.). BBC Bitesize. https://www.bbc.co.uk/bitesize/guides/z9jpn39/revision/2

224. Hiroshima Peace Memorial Museum. (n.d.). http://hpmmuseum.jp/?lang=eng

225. Wijegoonawardana, N. (2021). Peace education: Lessons from post-war Japan. International Journal of Research – Granthaalayah, 9(5), 290. https://granthaalayahpublication.org/journals/granthaalayah/article/download/3941/3987?inline=1

226. The Nagasaki atomic bomb and nature. (n.d.). Google Arts & Culture. https://artsandculture.google.com/story/the-nagasaki-atomic-bomb-and-nature-nagasaki-atomic-bomb-museum/rAXRxdk4LQAA8A?hl=en

227. Harry Truman's decision to use the atomic bomb. (n.d.). National Park Service. https://www.nps.gov/articles/trumanatomicbomb.htm

228. Stewards, G. (n.d.). Nature Quotes - Connecting to and Learning from Nature. Www.globalstewards.org.

https://www.globalstewards.org/connect-to-nature-quotes.htm

ABOUT US

modern daily. PRESS

Modern Daily Press focuses on crafted material especially for kids through subjects that captivate young minds - think action, adventure, and everything that sparks their curiosity!

Our commitment to producing high-quality content reflects our dedication to nurturing the love for reading and learning. Our team of passionate writers, editors, and illustrators work tirelessly to create books that not only entertain but also inspire.

From tales of epic battles to thrilling military adventures, we're on a mission to provide books that have the power to shape young minds.

Click the +Follow button on our Author Page join us as we embark on a journey of exploration and stay updated on our latest releases!

www.ingramcontent.com/pod-product-compliance
Ingram Content Group UK Ltd.
Pitfield, Milton Keynes, MK11 3LW, UK
UKHW020737300626
13456UKWH00025B/401